Debt or Democracy

Debt or Democracy

Public Money for Sustainability and Social Justice

Mary Mellor

PlutoPress
www.plutobooks.com

First published 2016 by Pluto Press
345 Archway Road, London N6 5AA

www.plutobooks.com

British Library Cataloguing in Publication Data
A catalogue record for this book is available from the British Library

ISBN   978 0 7453 3555 1   Hardback
ISBN   978 0 7453 3554 4   Paperback
ISBN   978 1 7837 1717 0   PDF eBook
ISBN   978 1 7837 1719 4   Kindle eBook
ISBN   978 1 7837 1718 7   EPUB eBook

This book is printed on paper suitable for recycling and made from fully managed
and sustained forest sources. Logging, pulping and manufacturing processes are
expected to conform to the environmental standards of the country of origin.

Typeset by Stanford DTP Services, Northampton, England
Text design by Melanie Patrick

Simultaneously printed in the European Union and United States of America

CONTENTS

Introduction

A system that is based ... on the ability of profit-seeking institutions to create money as a by-product of often grotesquely irresponsible lending is irretrievably unstable ... ordinary tax payers are being forced to suffer in order to save a banking system that has brought them only excess and ruin. This is intolerable: indeed a form of debt slavery ... No industry should have the capacity to inflict economic costs that may even surpass those of a world war.

Martin Wolf, Deputy Editor and Chief Economics Commentator,
Financial Times, London (2014: 350)

Following election defeat in 2010 the outgoing British Labour Chief Secretary to the Treasury left what was meant to be a humorous note for his successor: 'I'm afraid there is no money – with kind regards and good luck.' This note was subsequently portrayed by the victorious Conservative-Liberal Democrat government as a confession of financial profligacy that justified the imposition of austerity to 'balance the books'. At the same time, the Bank of England was making potentially unlimited new publicly created money available to the banking sector. Why were private financial institutions being supported by public money while public institutions were being starved of funds or privatised? How could one arm of the state have run out of money when another arm appeared to have unlimited amounts? This is the question I want to address in this book. Why was there public money for the banks but none for the people?

'Where is the money to come from?' 'Who is going to pay?' are some of the most politically debilitating questions. Proposals seeking to achieve environmental sustainability, social justice or other progressive policies are rejected by the implication that money is in short supply. Public expenditure is presented as zero sum. Somebody has to pay. Any public expenditure must therefore be at the expense of the individualised 'taxpayer' or private 'wealth creators', who are assumed to be reluctant to part with their money. Public expenditure then becomes politically problematic. However, public expenditure need not be zero sum; public money is not in short supply. The outpourings of new money to meet the financial crisis did not have a 'bottom line'. As the head of the European Central Bank declared, he would 'do what it takes'. Why did the banking sector trigger such largesse when the poor and vulnerable and the planet did not? While the people were subject to austerity, the financial sector quickly got the bonus culture rolling again.

Public Money for Private Rescue

Following the 2007–8 financial crisis, governments and public monetary authorities around the world pumped huge amounts of money into their banking sectors. Banks were supported or nationalised, toxic debts purchased, bank deposits guaranteed and cheap money made available. Governments ended up spending much more than they could raise in taxes to bail out their banking sector through loans, investment capital, or outright nationalisation. Central banks released high levels of 'liquidity', that is, they made new money available to support failing banks. By 2009, US government and central bank action had totalled $10.5 trillion (Wolf 2014: 361), and Wray calculates that by 2012 the US federal reserve could have allocated as much as $29 trillion in loans and various other forms of support to the US banking sector (2012: 89). This is nearly twice US GDP. Britain and Ireland had to offer similar levels of support to steady their banking and financial sectors. Ireland in particular publicly guaranteed all bank deposits. Felix Martin suggests that the crisis overall may end up costing more than three times global GDP (2014: 303).

Making such huge sums available didn't mean that they were spent or lost. By being made available they prevented the threatened collapse. However, the proportion that was spent and the subsequent economic downturn caused severe problems for governments. The extra expenditure was compounded by a collapse in tax revenue so that public deficits increased dramatically. In the US the annual deficit went from under 3 per cent of GDP to around 13 per cent between

2007 and 2009 (Wolf 2014: 30). As a consequence, overall state debt rose; in the case of the UK from just over 40 per cent of GDP in 2007 to over 80 per cent by 2014. Rather than being grateful for such extensive public rescue, mainstream economic opinion turned on governments, accusing them of profligate expenditure and burdening future taxpayers with unpayable debt. Austerity was imposed as states sought to eliminate deficits and cut public debt, with the heaviest impact on the poorest and most vulnerable, particularly in Britain.

While political attention was largely directed to increases in government expenditure, less attention was paid to the much more substantial sums of money made available by the central banks. Unlike government expenditure, the ability of central banks to spend such large sums of money was not challenged. Although it was being 'spent' with an uncertain expectation of being returned, the central banks were not seen as borrowing the money they dispensed and therefore it did not contribute to totals of state debt. This is because central banks have the privilege of being able to create money. More than that, they are expected to create money. They are seen as the source of public currency for the whole banking system. Why, then, are they not a source of public currency for the people? This question is central to the choice between debt and democracy.

Debt or Democracy

It is not contentious that public monetary authorities have exclusive control over the issue and circulation of national currencies. It is one of the most closely guarded national privileges, particularly for bank notes and coin (cash). As I will show, this right to create the public currency descends from the autocratic powers of rulers. The question is, why has it come to rest with central banks, rather than with states more generally? More importantly, how has this power been made available to the banking sector and not the people?

The problem with issuing new publicly created money through the banking sector is that it is only accessible as loans. As a result, the public currency supply has been privatised as debt. New public money only emerges when governments, businesses and individuals take on more debt. The main response to the crisis was therefore to pump more money into the banks hoping to get the great lending machine going again. Unfortunately, the main borrowers were in the financial sector itself, driving asset inflation, mortgages and speculation.

A money supply based on debt must end in crisis if debts can no longer be sustained. Banks had to be rescued not just because they were too big to fail; they were also too central to the creation and supply of the public currency. Even investment banks that were not supposed to directly interact with the public money supply had to be rescued, because they were so tied in to the banks' debt machine. This lesson was learnt when Lehman Brothers, the fourth-largest investment bank in the US, was allowed to fail. It had no automatic public guarantee as it was not a high street bank that took customer deposits with the obligation to refund them. It took only investor's money which was supposed to be subject to risk. However, the supply of national (and international) currencies had become so entangled with financial investment, borrowing and speculation, that Lehman's collapse threatened to take the whole commercially based money supply system down with it. Without large-scale, prompt, public action an unstoppable run on the largely insolvent banks could have been triggered.

The supply of new public money does not need to be circulated only as debt. When central banks create new money they do not borrow it from anyone: it is debt free at the point of creation. In fact, this is how I define public money. It is money that does not have any other origin – it is created by fiat, that is, on public authority alone. This meaning of public money must be distinguished from public funds perceived as money extracted by governments from the wider economy through taxation. Public money in this book refers to *new* money created by public monetary authorities. The crucial question is how does this money only become available through debt? That is a political question. There is no 'natural' way for public money to enter the economy. Whether it is spent, lent or allocated is a political choice. But it is one that people are not aware can be made. Why is there no democratic framework for the creation and circulation of that most public of institutions, the public currency? Worse, the public sector is seen as just another borrower. There is no public right to public money.

What the 2007–8 crisis shows is that if there is to be meaningful democracy in modern societies, there needs to be public debate about the balance between private control of, and public responsibility for, the monetary system. The size of the bailout by central banks and governments shows how dependent the banking and financial sector is upon publicly created money and public expenditure in a crisis. However, it is the public that then ends up in debt.

Public Debts and Deficits

While central bank support for the banking sector met with very little public comment or criticism, the position was very different for governments. When the budgetary impact stemming from the crisis drove them into deficit, there was an adverse political reaction. This is because they were deemed to be borrowing the money they spent, even when they were drawing on newly created money from the central bank. The public origin of this money was obscured by the claim that it is a debt that the public must repay. Given the debt relationship is between two arms of the state, who are the public in debt to? Are they not in debt to themselves?

This confusion occurs because central banks hover between the state and the banking sector. They are bankers to both. As I explore in Chapter 5, central banks are Janus-faced, combining the sovereign power of money creation and the commercial face of lending. I will argue that this confusion of roles has been central to the privatisation of the public money supply. The dilemma of government 'borrowing' publicly created money is resolved by the central bank selling the government debt to the wider banking and financial sector. In effect this means that the public are indebted to the very sector they are rescuing.

I will argue that the notion of public debt is largely an illusion reflecting the way that public money systems have been privatised in capitalist economies and the particular way central banks have developed. Deficits do not increase public debt if they are financed by new money. I will make the case that new money is continually being created by public authorities as they spend and by commercial banks as they make loans. While money created by banks always becomes a debt to the bank for the borrower, money created by public monetary authorities is not owed to anyone or by anyone. Declaring this public money to be a debt reflects the ideological economics of capitalism and the privatisation of the public money supply as a commercial commodity.

As discussed in Chapter 2, the history of money, and contemporary examples of social money systems, reveal a very different concept of money than that employed by conventional economics. Far from the public sector being dependent on the so-called wealth-creating sector, I will argue that the private sector is parasitical on the public capacity to create and guarantee the public currency. Central banks, with their ambivalent status between the commercial banking sector and the state, are in reality a symbol of the failure of commercial banking to create sustainable monetary structures. In fact, it is not only when it is in crisis that the banking and financial sector is dependent on public money. It also relies on the social and public nature of money in its daily workings. Socially trusted and publicly authorised money is essential if profits are to be realised in commercial exchange and capital is to be accumulated. The critical question is who owns and controls the supply of that money? The privatisation of money in capitalist economies means the private sector has developed a stranglehold on the public sector through the actual and ideological control of public funding. This I describe as 'handbag economics'.

Handbag Economics

Public services, public welfare and public infrastructure are all under attack from the ideology of 'handbag economics'. A handbag (purse) is here seen as symbolic of the public, as a 'housewife' dependent on an allowance from the capitalist 'head of household'. Handbag economics constantly reiterates a 'public as household' analogy that is rarely contradicted by mainstream opponents. All public activity is portrayed as a drain on the 'wealth creators', taken to mean the private economic sector, or the 'taxpayer', taken to be a purely private individual. All public funding is assumed to have been extracted by taxing the private sector. That this is a false view is clearly demonstrated by the huge outpourings of new public money from central banks in the face of the 2007–8 crisis.

However, given the dominance of handbag economic ideology, the rescue money has been represented as either public debt, money that the state has 'borrowed' from the sector it is rescuing, or as just a technical creation of public money by central banks to deal with the specifics of the banking crisis. As a result, while money is poured into the banking sector, the public is subjected to austerity and the assets and institutions of the public sector are stripped bare (Hudson 2013). Nevertheless, despite the attack on public funding, the public capacity to create and spend money has not ceased to exist. Instead, it has been suppressed through the 'independence' of the central banks from democratic governance, and derided as 'printing money' – unless it is to rescue the banks.

One of the triumphs of handbag economics is its main bag-carrier TINA: There Is No Alternative. While I will argue that there are many alternatives, TINA correctly represented the situation at the time of the banking and financial crisis. There was no effective challenge to handbag economics – there was, quite literally, no alternative. The left had an analysis of productive capitalism, even of finance capitalism, but it had no analysis that could respond to a crisis of money itself. One of the weakest areas of opposition was the lack of an alternative conception of the role of money and banking. Although there had been many voices analysing and critiquing the money and banking system over the previous hundred or so years, not least Keynes, progressive movements and parties had not picked this up. Questions about the supply of public currency, its creation and circulation, have been largely ignored by both right and left. Both see it as secondary to 'real' economic forces, that is, the capitalist market. For the left, the whole discussion is an irrelevance to the wider critique of capitalism. This is unfortunate, as the history of money fits well with the Marxian framework, as I will show. However, in mitigation, the monetary critiques come from a wide range of political perspectives: from radical calls for the democratisation of the money supply to right-wing demands for an equivalent to the gold standard.

The case for a politics of money is that far from spreading wealth, the privatisation of the money supply and the financialisation of society have led to a dramatic increase in inequality and the growth of fabulously wealthy financial elites. As governments lost control of their money systems and became trapped by them, the public lost faith in political democracy. Enormous financial wealth flowed around the world, paralysing government capacity to use tax as a means of redistribution. Instead of contributing to the welfare of society, the financial rich were profiting through investment in state debt: 'by replacing tax revenue with debt, governments contributed further to inequality, in that they offered secure investment opportunities to those whose money they would or could no longer confiscate and had to borrow instead' (Streeck 2014: 43). As Streeck points out, as state debt rose, democratic participation fell. The sense that there was no alternative led to disillusionment that political participation would have any effect. Worse, the public were responsible for a monetary system they could not control; they faced austerity to support the integrity of the monetary and fiscal regime. But if the people as a whole are held responsible for the money issued in their name, the public currency, they should have a democratic right to determine how that money is used.

In recent years, radical theories around money have developed a depth of analysis better fitting the reality of modern money and finance that is pushing at the door of a failed neoclassical economics and neoliberal philosophy. Drawing on historical and contemporary monetary analysis, I will put forward a radical perspective on money that challenges capitalism and conventional economics. It will open up the possibility of creating an economic democracy that is based on green and egalitarian principles.

For this, an understanding of money is necessary.

Understanding Money

Money is something of which nearly everyone has immediate knowledge. Most people would not leave the house without money, and children often receive pocket money at an early age. Not having money creates a severe social, economic and political disadvantage. However, identifying what money actually is and what it does, is more difficult. Its form may be represented by coins, notes, plastic cards, bank or mobile phone data or a range of other forms from stones to wooden sticks. In terms of functions, economic textbooks generally list money as acting as a medium of exchange or payment, as a way of measuring relative values and as a store of value over time. There is considerable debate about what these mean in practice and which are the most important. However, the basic concerns here are not just what money is or does, but how its form and supply are controlled. In conventional economic thinking this question is rarely asked. Money is assumed to appear in the economy as commercial necessity demands: that economic activity somehow creates money. This presupposition leads to the assumption that having money is evidence of having created some form of economic value. The rich deserve their wealth because they must have done something to have earned it.

This benign view of the rich would be very different if they were known to be, directly or indirectly, able to simply create that money. In reality, rather than competing for a fixed stock of money where the winner was assumed to have been the most effective, efficient or productive, the wealthy have merely expanded the money supply with themselves as beneficiaries. It is not without note that the vast expansion of the financial sector and its culture of huge bonuses were accompanied by a dramatic increase in money supply. Total bank balances were exceeding GDP many times over, most notably in Iceland and Ireland. Even several years after the crisis the state-rescued Royal Bank of Scotland (RBS) had a balance sheet equivalent to UK GDP.

Money is Social and Public

My focus in this book is public money, that is, the creation and circulation of the public currency by public authorities. Currency is often taken to just mean cash, notes and coin, but I will take it to include all forms of money that people readily accept in payment: credit or debit cards and transfers between bank accounts using various forms of technology. In modern economies there is a contradictory approach to how money is created and circulated. While it is accepted that public monetary authorities create and control the public currency, money is also seen as being 'made' in commercial activities. Under handbag economics the commercial role of money is seen as the most important. While not disputing the centrality of money to commerce, I want to rescue the social and public nature of money.

Although money has a long social and public history, conventional economics tends to see it as a natural adjunct to the market. This is justified by the assumption that the origin of money was linked to both precious metal and commerce. As I will show in Chapter 4, the history of money reveals that it did not emerge from trade or gold; it is much older and broader than both. Historically it has been created and used in social and political contexts as much as in commercial ones. Early histories indicate that traditional societies had forms of money for social purposes such as injury payments, dowries or tribute. Military societies such as Rome used money for imperial conquest. Theocracies used money systems to build and fund temples and priesthoods. There are also many contemporary examples of people creating new forms of money such as local or internet currencies. Rather than emerging 'naturally', money systems are built on social custom or public authority; they are social and political constructs. Even today, the public currency in all its forms relies on social and public trust. People trust that bits of metal, paper, plastic and bank records will be honoured by others when presented.

While social money depends on traditional customary use, or newly adopted social agreement, as in the case of contemporary local money schemes, modern forms of money are mainly represented by public currencies supported by public authority. Public authority here embraces monetary institutions such as central banks and state treasuries but also the wider public itself who honour the publicly designated currency (that is, the authorised currency in all its forms) by supplying the labour, goods, services and resources it represents.

Public reaction to bank failure shows that depositors themselves see the money system as a state, and therefore a public, responsibility. When in 2007 the British bank Northern Rock found itself the dead canary in the coalmine heralding the future crash, the bank's chief executive unsuccessfully tried to stop the bank run, as did the Governor of the Bank of England. Only when the Chancellor of the Exchequer, Alistair Darling, put the full authority of the state behind the bank did the crowds disperse. If securing the banking system is demonstrably a public responsibility, should not banks be seen as part of the public sector? For Martin, banks should be seen more as a civil service where 'the ultimate goal of monetary policy isn't monetary stability, or financial stability but a just and prosperous society ... monetary policy is intensely political ... it is a technology of government' (2014: 272).

Democratising Money

My starting point is that money systems and their currencies are of necessity public and social. As such, they should be democratically accountable. Treating money purely as a commodity and monopolising its creation through bank loans means that the majority of people can only access money through wage labour or debt. There is no public *right* to money, and wealth is defined only as the outcome of profit-seeking activity. Failure to labour threatens the removal of livelihood rights. People without work must be punished or vilified, even if there are no suitable jobs, or they have personal difficulties. Commercial activities must continue even in the face of environmental threats. Social, communal, familial and public activities are not valued in themselves because they are not traded for profit. Inequality is welcomed, as the rich are assumed to provide employment through their investments and consumption.

These assumptions are undermined if the necessity of public money to capitalist finance is revealed. I will argue that it is not private wealth and private money that drives prosperity, but public money and public wealth that creates the framework for private profit. If environmental sustainability and social justice are to be achieved, public money must be reclaimed to support social and public provision of goods and services in the same way it has been used to save the financial system.

Reclaiming the creation and direct issue of public money would change the role of taxation. Rather than tax being a source of revenue to enable public funding as it is now perceived, it would become a mechanism to retrieve money that had already been spent. Taxation would remove money from circulation to balance expenditure on goods and services that were free at the point of use. Rather than 'taking money out of the taxpayer's pocket', public expenditure would put money into that pocket and then ask for a portion back. Tax would, however, still be used to harness commercially created money, to change behaviour (such as less resource use) and to redistribute wealth. Funding public expenditure out of democratically controlled public money would remove the need to prioritise the creation of commodity value in the pursuit of profit as a prerequisite of public benefit. As will be argued in Chapter 2, public money could be distributed and used for the circulation of use value, that is, the exchange of goods and services without a profit motive.

At present there exists a socially and ecologically wasteful two-step economy. People have to labour at whatever work they can find, in order to provide for the things they need. Expenditure in the public sector depends on money being 'made' in the commercial sector. Unfortunately, work that makes a profit need be neither useful nor necessary. A one-step economy would aim to bring together as far as possible the work people do and the things they need. Acknowledgement of the existence and capabilities of public money would enable wealth to be created first in the social or public sector. Public services would be a source of new money that could then circulate in the social, public or commercial sector. What makes the difference here is the conception of what money is and how it is used; the definition of wealth and how it is created as will be discussed in Chapter 2.

Reclaiming money as a public resource could be the basis on which economic democracy could be built as it breaks the stranglehold of TINA economics. Economic democracy through the social and public use of money is a clear alternative to personal and public indebtedness to the commercial sector. The clear choice is between a money system based on bank debt and public control of a debt-free money supply. Democratic control of money creation and circulation would release people from the debt-encumbered commercial money system and establish the basis for a public economy that could enable a socially just and ecologically sustainable means of provisioning for the people as a whole.

As discussed in Chapter 3, the democratisation of money would require an expansion of public participation that is much wider than the state or the governing regime. It could also lead to a challenge to neoliberal assertions of the superiority of the commercial sector and to existing patterns of ownership and control of resources and wealth. Reversing the privatisation of money would undermine one of the main mechanisms of capitalist accumulation and create the means of independent public provisioning. The 2007–8 financial crisis raises fundamental questions about the nature of money and how it is controlled. It reveals that the sovereign power of money creation has been harnessed in the service of the banking sector rather than the people. The time has come for the people to claim that sovereign right and replace debt by democracy.

Outline of the Book

The first chapter will set out the main assumptions behind the privatisation of the money supply, the attack on public finance, and the politics of austerity. The next two chapters will set out the core proposals presented in this book. The second chapter challenges the mainstream views of the TINA economy by exploring alternative conceptions and examples of ways in which egalitarian and not-for-profit provisioning systems have been organised. Its starting point is a socially just and ecologically sustainable approach that stresses the principles of sufficiency and equality. The third chapter will look in detail at the concept of public money and how a democratised politics of money could achieve the aims set out in the previous chapter. The rest of the book supplies the background to the proposals set out in the Chapter 3.

Chapter 4 will argue that TINA and handbag economics are based on the false foundation of four myths and a confusion. The four myths are (1) that the state cannot or should not create money; (2) that money emerged in the context of trade; (3) that money originated in precious metal; (4) that banks act as intermediaries between savers and borrowers. The confusion is about the role of central banks in relation to the public and private creation and circulation of money. The whole book is concerned with the first myth, Chapter 4 will discuss the other three myths, while Chapter 5 looks at the confusion around the role of central banks.

While radical theories and analyses of money and banking inform the earlier chapters, these will be explored more fully in relation to public conceptions of money in Chapter 6. Although most of the discussion in the book addresses public money in the context of a single monetary authority or monetary union, the seventh chapter will discuss the difficult area of democratic control of monetary arrangements between monetary systems. The concluding chapter will explore how the arguments and proposals in the book contribute to the critique of capitalism and the case for radical social change.

1

The Privatisation of Money and the Politics of Austerity

A core organising principle of modern economic life is a publicly recognised money system. This is represented by a national currency (dollars, pounds, yen) but cross-national currencies are also possible, most notably the euro. The essence of a publicly recognised money system is that economic transactions are conducted with reference to that currency either in immediate terms (payment by cash) or through a record of debt or payment (electronic transfer, cheque). In this sense all money is public where there is general acceptance of the money form backed up by law or public monetary authorities. A public currency authorised as 'legal tender' also involves restrictions on how that money can be created and circulated. Cash, that is public currency represented as notes and coin, is usually the monopoly of public monetary authorities. Private unlicensed production would be prosecuted as counterfeiting.

While the legal basis for the creation and circulation of cash is generally clear cut, the position for records of money value and transfer is not. In modern economies non-cash forms of money, mainly bank records, far outstrip actual cash. The legal status of this wider use of public currency is more problematic as non-cash records can be both publicly and privately created. While the notion of public currency is usually taken to mean notes and coin, in practice commercially created bank accounts also act as a public currency in the sense that transfers between them are accepted in payment. What then, counts as money? This is not an easy question to answer. Monetary authorities have struggled with calculations of M0, M1, M2, M3, M4, etc. This runs from only counting cash, reserves and current accounts to various forms of savings and other monetary instruments. While calculating the amount of money in circulation is relatively simple if this just means cash (notes and coin), when bank deposit accounts are added in, savings accounts, bank vault reserves, central bank reserves, assets easily convertible to cash and so on, the position becomes highly complex.

In this book money will be defined as a generally accepted and publicly authorised representation of nominal value with reference to which social, public and commercial obligations and entitlements can be conducted. As a representation, money can take many forms both tangible and intangible, and its use is not solely commercial. Money can represent family commitments such as gifts, dowries, inheritance. It can represent civic or public commitments such as fines, rewards, taxes as well as trade-related activities. Private forms of money can also be created, such as digital currencies like Bitcoin or local currencies such as the Bristol pound. However while these are currencies that members of the public have created, they are not the public currency. They are not formally authorised and used by the public as a whole. The privatisation of money in this chapter does not refer to the creation of private monies, but to privatisation of the *public* currency. It focuses on the ability of banks to create and circulate new public currency as a commercial act: making a loan.

The creation and circulation of new money is rarely discussed in economic textbooks. Money is mainly taken to be an existing aspect of economic processes. Moreover, there is often assumed to be a fixed stock of money that circulates between households, firms and governments. Money is seen as passive, merely acting as a mirror of the 'real' economy of production and consumption. The idea that the creation and circulation of new money can be an independent force in social, public and commercial processes is rarely considered. Once the active agency of money is raised, the question of the politics of money becomes critical. Who owns and controls money? What are the implications of the privatisation of the public currency? How has it been privatised?

The most straightforward assumption would be that public authorities create the public currency. Technically this is true for cash, but this book is much more concerned with the bulk of money in circulation, non-cash money records, predominantly bank accounts. In the UK cash makes up only about 3 per cent of the public currency in circulation. How the remaining 97 per cent is created and circulated becomes the critical question. Neoliberal economic ideology is quite clear about who does not, and should not, create that money: the state. States must not 'print money' – unless it is to service the banking and financial sector. Who then, can and does create money? This is the question that neoliberal theory ignores. However the logic of the neoliberal position would mean that, in the absence of a public role in the creation and circulation of money, only the private financial sector is left, or more specifically, the banks. As will be discussed more fully in later chapters, the emergence of capitalism saw a shift from domination of the creation and circulation of money by sovereign rulers to domination by the commercial financial sector.

Control of the public money supply by the banking sector has a major implication. Regardless of the ownership structure of the bank (public, co-operative, commercial), banks can only create money in one way: as debt. Companies, individuals, governments must all borrow new money into circulation. This puts the banking sector, and thus the commercial sector in capitalist economies, into the driving seat but also creates a contradiction at the heart of the money system. Money based on debt is socially, ecologically and economically unsustainable. Debt puts pressure on individuals as borrowers, increases damage to, and commodification of, the environment, and ultimately implodes economically when people and organisations can take no more debt, or banks can find no creditworthy borrowers.

The privatisation of the public money supply as debt in modern economies can be traced back to the origins of modern banking systems, as will be argued in Chapter Four. However, there are three features of modern money and banking that facilitated a shift in the balance between the public and private creation of money to an almost exclusive creation of money through bank-issued debt. The first, largely unintended feature is the changing way in which money is represented in contemporary societies, mainly as bank or other accounts rather than as cash. The second more important feature is ideological: the attack on the public creation of public money ('states must not print money') and the rise of neoliberal market fundamentalism and 'handbag economics'. The third is the change in structural conditions: financialisation and globalisation.

The Decline of Cash

Although the most recognisable form of public currency, cash (notes and coin), is monopolised by public monetary authorities, towards the end of the twentieth century in the richer economies it was increasingly less used. If people are happy to operate entirely within the banking system for their accounts and transfers of money, the production of cash by the Treasury or the central bank becomes unnecessary. In fact, using or holding large amounts of cash can be seen as a sign of possible illegal activity or tax evasion. Almost by default, the money system was being privatised as the creation and circulation of currency became dominated by banks' role in money transfer and commercial lending. There was little general concern for, or even awareness of, the consequences of this shift in money supply even though it meant that nearly all new money was created as debt. The shift to cashless financial transactions is, however, not universal. In India in 2013, for example, 95 per cent of transactions were still in cash. However, cash use is also being replaced in many countries with under-developed banking systems by mobile phone transfers that may have a similar impact on the balance between the public and private control of the creation and circulation of money.

Neoliberalism and Market Fundamentalism

The ideological attack on public control of the creation and circulation of money is based on neoliberal market fundamentalism. Cash must only be produced in response to demand from the banking sector. Markets are the sole creators of wealth, therefore only the market can provide an income for household and public expenditure. Public expenditure is dependent on money generated through commercial value and commercial activities. States are seen as inefficient competitors for scarce resources, particularly money. The dominance of neoclassical economics led nearly all mainstream political parties to accept the emphasis on the microeconomics of individual choice as the basis of modern economies. The only role for state monetary authorities was to maintain the value of money, that is, prevent inflation.

Market fundamentalism meant that economic priorities were left in the hands of individual and commercial decision-making. The Keynesian macroeconomic view that governments were responsible for the overall management of the economy was roundly defeated. Governments no longer had an ameliorative economic role. States were inefficient and impeded competitiveness. Nationalised industries were privatised, public services outsourced. The language of opposition was lost as governments competed to 'restructure' the labour market and restrict worker rights, free up companies from 'red tape', cut taxation and create 'incentives' for commercial expansion and privatisation. The Keynesian commitment to full employment was abandoned and replaced with a neoliberal demand for deregulation and small government. Financial sector priorities dominated both government and the non-financial sector using the rationale of shareholder value maximisation. This change was accomplished via increased actual and threatened use of hostile takeovers, hedge fund activism, and increased use of massive stock option awards for top management (Palley 2013b:75). Leveraged buyouts burdened firms with unprecedented levels of debt; demands for short-term high rates of return undercut long-term investment. Financial advantage drove business off-shore breaking the link with community and country.

The concept of the public itself as an economic actor, let alone the idea of a public role in money creation, was totally rejected. As a result, the idea of public investment, public service and the creation of public wealth was marginalised in both theory and practice in most contemporary economies. Instead, the privatised domination of money issue and circulation emerged virtually unchallenged. It became the heart of TINA – there is no alternative. If all wealth is created by the private sector, there is no role for the public except as an impediment to growth and prosperity. A profligate public sector is seen as putting a heavy burden on the 'wealth creators' and the 'taxpayer', who are considered to be the only source of money and wealth in the economy.

Representing all public expenditure as 'taxpayer's money' creates an alienating division between the citizen as taxpayer and the citizen as a member of the public. The anti-public rhetoric derided wasteful government departments, inefficient public services and work-shy, lead-swinging recipients of welfare. The ideology was so strong that even though in the UK welfare recipients other than pensioners represented only a small percentage of the welfare budget, harsh measures such as the 'bedroom tax' (loss of benefit for having 'extra' bedrooms) could be imposed on families and people with disabilities. Harsh benefit rules also meant that sanctions or delayed decisions left people without any form of income for weeks on end. Food banks became a regular feature of many people's lives including the working poor. As John Weeks argues, the crisis resulted from a 'Big Market Lie' supported by the ideology propounded by the 'pseudointellectual abstractions of the fakeconomics profession' (2014: 60). Neoclassical claims that perfect competitive markets could exist were negated by the evidence that real markets were far from perfect. Market fundamentalism also ignored all the evidence that public expenditure has been essential to most of the technological developments behind much commercial activity (Mazzucato 2013).

In the climate of the last decades of the twentieth century, neoliberal thinking triumphed. Global markets were opened up with the free flow of production and capital (but not labour). States were to be rolled back and minimised. Countervailing institutions such as trades unions were restricted. Political parties shifted to free market policies and the public responded by not voting, creating a 'democratic deficit' reflecting the cynical assumption that 'they are all as bad as each other'. Citizens became consumers. Employee rights became zero hours contracts. Welfare support became scrounging. Houses became investment opportunities. Debt became a way of life. The state became a dependent 'household'.

Handbag Economics and the 'Public as Household' Analogy

'Handbag economics' sees the public sector as analogous to a household, dependent upon external sources of income. Like a thrifty housewife limited to spending only what is in her purse, states are expected to minimise their expenditure, and most definitely not spend more than their income, or borrow to cover any shortfall. In the absence of any alternative source of money the public household is seen as solely dependent on the private 'wealth-creating' sector. The supply of money to the public sector must therefore originate with the taxpayer or the money markets (public borrowing).

However, under handbag economics the public household is in a much more constrained position than actual households. Whereas actual households are encouraged to borrow extensively provided they can afford the repayments, any borrowing by the public household is condemned by handbag economics. The ideal is for states to be in surplus, but at minimum they should 'balance the books', 'pay their way', 'live within their means'. The case is made that as all debt and interest payments are a burden on the taxpayer, now or in the future, the public sector must be limited as to how much can be borrowed (overall debt) or how far current expenditure can exceed income (deficit). Preferably states should have no borrowing at all and certainly no deficit.

In the late twentieth century the public as household analogy became the commonsense of the age. It found resonance with the public and lay behind the major attack on the state that enabled neoliberal socioeconomic changes: market fundamentalism, globalisation, labour market flexibility. Under handbag ideology, public institutions were privatised or their activities put out to competitive tender on the grounds that the private sector was more efficient and therefore would cost less. Privatisation of public assets and private investment in public assets and services were seen as the route to prosperity. Rather than reflecting a true analogy with actual households, which would be more like the Keynesian model of borrowing when necessary, it became clear that the real aim of the household analogy was to shrink the public sector. The demand for small government was particularly strong in the Anglo-American economies. In the UK this resulted in such widespread privatisation of public resources and organisations that it became a 'private island' (Meek 2014).

Extensive outsourcing of public services was an economic model supported by most mainstream political parties. Huge private companies were paid to provide public services across the globe, from immigration detention centres to speed cameras, community health services, prisons, transport services, school inspections, air traffic control, welfare adjudication and payments and many more. Critics argue that while outsourcing tends to reduce the immediate costs of public services, the 'efficiencies' achieved often amount to cutting pay and services in the long run (Funnell et al. 2009). The neoliberal project of privatising public services also saw mounting examples of performance failure, most notably in providing security for the London Olympics in 2012, forcing the government to bring in the army. Other UK examples included the failure to provide adequate out of hours home-based medical (GP) services in Cornwall, offender tagging contractors who charged for non-existent tags, job seeker companies who did not find jobs, and disability checking companies who were subject to high numbers of successful appeals.

Monitoring effectiveness was difficult as firms could hide behind claims of commercial confidentiality. Margaret Hodge MP, Chair of the UK Parliament Public Accounts Committee, is reported as saying that what is happening is 'the development of quasi-monopoly private providers ... we don't really understand the size of their empires ... It's a new phenomenon': 'What is becoming really clear to me ... is that [private sector providers] – they're good at winning contracts, but too often, they're bad at running services' (*Guardian*, 30 July 2013). As well as privatising public services, there also seems to be a growing 'publicisation' of commercial companies that depend heavily on public contracts for their survival.

Structural Changes

Although the attack on the state was mainly ideological, it did reflect macroeconomic changes that undermined the Keynesian compromise between state and market. Forces came together that led in the early 1970s to 'stagflation', low growth, high unemployment and inflation, which economic theory at the time claimed could not co-exist. One of the major structural changes was the collapse of the Bretton Woods system. The final remnants fell in 1971 when the American President Richard Nixon had to acknowledge that central banks around the world could no longer exchange dollars for gold. The admission that there was no intrinsic limit on the production of dollars (which did not work anyway – hence the collapse of the system) meant that all money became fiat money, that is, money that existed by public acceptance and authority alone. As there was no yardstick against which to fix exchange rates, currencies both floated and flowed.

The globalised spread of capitalist markets, global capital, off-shoring and tax avoidance and evasion also undermined public control over the business and financial sectors. Social and environmental standards fell by the wayside as wages were driven down and environmental standards lowered. The floating of exchange rates also led to insecurity in important global markets such as oil. The Oil Producing and Exporting Countries (OPEC) both restricted production and raised prices, dramatically increasing the costs of production in the older industrial countries which became uncompetitive. This led, in turn, to industrial conflict as employers tried to force down wage costs.

As industrial production faltered, financialisation became an engine of growth. Rather than investment in production, the investment of money in money, or in assets that only increased in financial terms, became increasingly predominant. Western banks and investors looking for new borrowers found ready takers in the newly developing countries. Initially, interest rates were reasonable and commodity markets seemed buoyant enough to enable repayment. However, a majority world debt crisis emerged when prices in commodity markets fell while the monetarist attempt to control inflation in the developed countries by increasing the price of money drove up interest rates. In the developed economies debts also rose in the following decades. This resulted in a sharp rise in money supply, much of it borrowed for financial investment or mortgage finance. Economies became skewed towards the financial sector and housing, particularly in the UK, where the attraction of investment to the new financial centre drove up the value of the currency making industrial production even less competitive.

Josef Huber points out that in the US between 1997 and 2007 only a fifth of the increased money supply went to what he describes as 'real income generation' while the rest went to consumption and asset inflation. In Germany the situation was even worse as only one eighth of the additional money produced real income growth (Huber 2014: 45). In the boom times, with the growing demand for home loans and other forms of personal debt, it seemed that almost anyone could take on debt. However, the main increase in borrowing came from the financial sector itself. 'Leverage', that is, debt, enabled financial investments to be 'levered' up generating high levels of profit. Finance capital became 'parasitic', feeding on debt-fuelled unsustainable growth (Hossein-zadeh 2014). The late twentieth and early twenty-first century saw a vast growth in speculation and complex financial instruments. These changes were enabled by relaxation of financial controls on both credit and capital flows, as the public controls of the financial system put in place in the decades after the Great Depression were gradually dismantled.

The Great Depression followed a boom based on uncontrolled lending and stock market speculation which ended in the Great Crash. The most emblematic example of public control of finance was the US Glass-Steagall Act of 1933 which separated deposit, transfer and personal loan banking from more speculative investment banking. Much of the Act was repealed by the Dodd-Frank Bank Modernisation Act in 1999. However, actual control had been slipping away for some time, particularly since the floating of most national currencies made global financial investment and speculation more lucrative. In Britain, credit and capital controls were lifted in the early 1970s, but the process was accelerated by the mid-1980s 'big bang' policies launched by the British Prime Minister Margaret Thatcher (doyen of both the handbag and handbag economics) and the US President Ronald Reagan. High street and investment banks got back into bed with each other, so much so that the collapse of Lehman Brothers in September 2008 nearly brought down much of the developed world banking sector.

The Route to Crisis

The era of TINA neoliberalism saw the money supply rise rapidly, particularly in the US and the UK, as the financial sector grew dramatically. Bank-issued debt was the main source of this expansion. Most of the new borrowing went to households and the financial sector, taking each to debts of over 100 per cent of GDP in the US and the UK. In many countries the balance sheet of the financial sector grew to many times GDP, up to 11 times in the case of Iceland. Even by 2013, assets on European banks' balance sheets still amounted to more than 350 per cent of total GDP and this was likely to require 'considerable public resources' to resolve (Botsch 2013: 21).

The debt-fuelled expansion of the financial sector led to asset price bubbles and an increasing share of investment and profits going to, and coming from, speculation and financial manipulation. While much of the growth in the financial sector was based on this 'leveraged' speculation, debt itself also became a commodity. Debt was bought, sold and insured in obscurely named 'instruments' such as structured investment vehicles, collateralised debt obligations and credit default swaps. Large 'wholesale' markets opened up in which financial institutions lent to each other. It was 'finance feeding finance' where banks were not only lending to other financial institutions but themselves borrowing from other banks and the wider money markets to support large-scale speculative 'proprietary' trading. Erturk and Solari calculate that proprietary trading, that is the bank trading directly on its own account rather than acting as an agent for external investors, accounted for two thirds of the revenues of Goldman Sachs and Lehmans (2007: 378). Writing presciently in 2007 they saw banks as 'not so much institutions as unstable experiments in opportunist innovation' compounded by the fact that 'nobody from the outside understands the sources of income in investment banking' (2007: 383). Eventually the whole structure of derivatives, securities and leverage imploded.

Financialisation had encouraged people to see themselves as financial agents with the promotion of 'people's capitalism' and easily available credit (Mellor 2010a: 58). People were encouraged to 'release' the 'equity' in their homes, that is, take out a second mortgage. Consumption, rather than production, became the prime mechanism of economic growth, again based on borrowing (Lawson 2009), while wages stagnated or even fell. During this time, debt became the mechanism by which many families sustained their lifestyle, often using the increasing asset value of their homes as security. The promotion of debt also featured in public policy where the solution to financial exclusion, a euphemism for the lack of money, was to provide access to debt through 'affordable credit' or microcredit. Inequality was also driven by the dramatic increases in income generated by the financial sector's bonus culture. While the majority of people saw their debts rise and their overall income fall, wealth 'trickled up to the lucky few'. It was growth for the few without prosperity for the many (Jackson 2009: 6). As Blyth argues, 'Global finance made so much hay, not through efficient markets but by riding up and down three interlinked giant global asset bubbles using huge amounts of leverage ... we may have impoverished a few million people to save an industry of dubious social utility that is now on its last legs' (2013: 232).

The lack of political concern about the escalating money supply reflected its failure to have any impact on high street inflation. Since the stagflation of the 1970s, a low target for inflation was the main focus of government macroeconomic policy. There were several interlinked factors that obscured the danger of inflation. Most importantly, the rapid price rises were in financial assets, including housing, which did not figure in measures of inflation. Very little of the money flowed into the wider economy as it stuck to the fingers of the very rich. The globalisation of production also saw a flood of cheap goods which kept consumer prices low. Any wider rises in commodity prices mainly impacted on poorer people and poorer countries. The fact that there was a high level of inflation in share prices and housing in the most prosperous countries was seen as a sign of increased wealth not instability.

The triumph of neoliberal handbag economics was the containment of the public and the liberation of the private. However, the financial sector did not repay its liberty with responsibility. As the crisis unravelled, evidence emerged of corruption, fraud, money laundering, insider trading and lending, conflicts of interest, mis-selling and manipulation of markets such as LIBOR (the price at which banks lend to each other) and FOREX (foreign exchange rates). However, even as the litany of misdemeanours became apparent, states still strove to get the debt-machine going again. Public money was thrown at the banking sector, but most of it piled up in bank reserves, enabling financial institutions to settle their own debts or invest in financial activities that saw the bonus culture reinvigorated.

While most commentators and governments were cheerleaders for the new experiments in finance, there were warnings. The Australian economist Steve Keen (2013) had long argued that private debt (personal and commercial) was much higher in the run up to the crisis than before the Great Depression. Keen and many other critics of neoliberal finance drew on the work of the late Hyman Minsky, who had pointed out the tendency to financial instability even in the best of circumstances. Minsky argued that the ultimate contradiction was that success must breed failure. To the extent that economies are built on debt they require confidence. Success, and particularly seemingly stable success, builds confidence. When things look good there is a tendency for borrowing to escalate to the point where there is not sufficient capacity or value in the economy to repay debts or even the interest. In the good times there is a tendency to overlook the possibility of optimism leading to more risky behaviour therefore creating instability (Nesvetailova 2007). Minsky pointed to the irony that the more stability the more the likelihood of instability. This was perfectly illustrated in the subprime housing crisis in the US where the fact that hardly anyone defaulted on their mortgages led to increasingly risky and fraudulent lending. Once the collapse occurs the only source of money to meet old debts is new borrowing. However, in a bust there is no basis for optimism, or what Keynes called animal spirits.

The dilemma for the privatisation of the public currency supply is that when borrowing collapses in a privatised money system so does the supply of public currency. When the 2007–8 crisis came the credit crunch saw a huge contraction in money supply as people paid off their debts where they could and financial assets lost their value. At this point public control of public money moved to centre stage. Unfortunately this did not dent the dominance of neoliberalism and handbag economics.

The Road to Austerity: Public Debts and Deficits

A major aspect of handbag economics is the demand that public expenditure should be limited to public income, taken to mean overall taxation. However, states have rarely been able to live within those restrictions for reasons that will be discussed in Chapter 5. Therefore in practice, in most years, states have a deficit, that is, a gap between income and expenditure. To bridge this gap states 'borrow' money (a concept which this book challenges) against future taxation. Public budgets are also structured so that, unlike commercial companies, public borrowing is not seen as investment. It is seen as an expense on current revenue. In the UK, this has led to distortions such as Private Finance Initiatives where private companies borrow on behalf of the public sector to fund major public investments. This keeps the loan off the government's accounts, even though this may involve much greater expenditure in the long run.

European monetary union and the Eurozone's central bank (ECB) were established at the height of neoliberal dominance. The influence of handbag economics produced EU rules limiting both public debts and deficits together with a purely commercial role for the central bank. States are to be limited to 60 per cent of GDP for state borrowing and 3 per cent of GDP for state deficits. According to the rules, the ECB cannot directly buy or administrate sovereign debt. It can create new public money but only in response to demand from the commercial banks. The ECB has spent a lot of money bailing out both the banking sector and sovereign debt, but this has mainly been in partnership with the European Union and the IMF. However, the threat of deflation saw the ECB embrace quantitative easing in 2015, several years after the Federal Reserve and the Bank of England. Quantitative easing puts money into the financial sector by directly buying financial assets, mainly government debt, rather than merely lending against those assets.

Handbag economics leads to what Nersisyan and Wray describe as 'deficit hysteria'. They point out that all US governments have accrued debt, except for 1835 when Jackson's government eliminated the national debt. This was followed by a deep recession in 1837 (2010: 116). The hysteria about government deficits, they argue, is due to a flawed understanding about how the monetary system works. In fact, as will be argued in this book, deficits are not a problem. On the contrary, a deficit is necessary – more public money must always be created and circulated than is reclaimed through taxation or debt repayment, otherwise there would be no money free of debt in circulation. Most importantly, the state should not extract more money than it spends. For the UK, Victoria Chick and Ann Pettifor point out that overall government expenditure reduces rather than increases public debt. They conclude that apart from the two world wars 'there is a very strong negative association between public expenditure and the public debt ... as public expenditure increases, public debt falls and vice versa' (2010: 2). In fact, the architects of neoliberal finance, British Prime Minister Margaret Thatcher and the US President Ronald Reagan, both generated deficits that by deficit hysteria standards would be seen as high.

The 2007–8 crisis saw both public debts and deficits increase as the costs of bank rescue and rising welfare expenditure were accompanied by a collapse in tax receipts as the recession bit. The first country to collapse under the pressure of the crisis was Greece, which seemed to justify the strictures of the EU rules on sovereign debt and deficit.

Greece: The Exception that Seemed to Justify the Rule

In 2010 the case against public expenditure and for austerity was greatly enhanced by the need for a bailout in Greece. It was one of the few European countries that went into the crisis with a high level of public debt at over 100 per cent of GDP (Italy was another). This compared with a European average of 66 per cent. A major factor in Greek state borrowing was the lack of effective taxation. Much of its economy was cash in hand while its wealthiest citizens avoided paying tax altogether. When it joined the Eurozone Greece appeared to meet the Maastricht criteria through creative accounting (reportedly helped by Goldman Sachs) that managed to get much of its debt off the government's balance sheet. Following the crisis its national debt had risen to over 140 per cent by 2010. As its economy had virtually collapsed together with its tax take, Greece was about to default on its debts.

This was a problem for Greece but also a problem for the banks which held that debt, mainly in France and Germany. Equally, many banks and financial institutions were threatened by insurances that had been taken out on the possibility of default, particularly in the US. This was enhanced by the ludicrous position where anyone could take a stake on the possibility of Greek sovereign debt default even if they did not hold any of the debt themselves. Possible Greek default was a problem for the financial sector well beyond its shores. In May 2010 Greece received the first of its bailouts and faced the full force of handbag economics, the imposing of severe austerity measures.

Public employees were sacked, businesses closed and unemployment rose dramatically to approaching a third of the population and more than half for young people. The people took the pain for five years. The economy shrank by 25 per cent. In January 2015 the people rebelled. Forty per cent of the vote in a snap general election went to a coalition of the left, Syriza, on an anti-austerity platform. There then followed a protracted series of negotiations with the Troika (the EU, ECB and IMF). The sticking point for Syriza was the unsustainability of the level of Greek debt and the lack of any growth strategy to enable repayment. Faced with the prospect of continued austerity, Syriza called a referendum in July 2015 in which more than 60 per cent of the voters rejected the Troika terms. In response the ECB placed restrictions on its liquidity support for the Greek banks triggering something Greece had not had: a banking crisis. Banks were closed with no immediate prospect of re-opening. This could be seen as a political act by the ECB, forcing the Greeks into a choice between submitting to an even harsher austerity programme or leaving the Eurozone.

A critical political problem was that the Eurozone's handbag economics projected a zero sum view of money that saw it as a limited resource. The two bailouts for Greece and the proposal for a third were deemed to be coming out of the pockets of Eurozone citizens. Eurozone leaders were unable to be more generous towards Greece for fear of a backlash from their own voters. This stemmed from the lack of a public monetary role for the ECB. As will be discussed in Chapter 5, the capacity to create money free of debt is a critical aspect of any central bank. It is a political decision to make this money only available to the banking sector. The failure to create a public monetary function for the Eurozone will tear it apart if it is not addressed. Without the capacity to create public money for public purposes, the Eurozone merely has a common commercial currency, not a public monetary union.

Far from justifying the Eurozone rules, Greece proved that austerity didn't work. Despite five years of severe cutbacks, the national debt had gone up, not down, as a percentage of GDP (140%–175%). This was mainly because GDP had collapsed and little inroad had been made on tax reform. Although Greece appeared to have excessive sovereign debt according to neoliberal views, this did not imply a high level of state expenditure. Before the crisis its public expenditure as a proportion of GDP was 54 per cent. This was exceeded by France and Finland while five other countries were over 50 per cent. Its tax take, however, was only 38 per cent (Wolf 2014: 46). Unlike the position in other countries needing a bailout, Greece did not have a severe crisis in either housing, personal debt or the banking sector. In most other cases of bailout a build-up of sovereign debt prior to the crisis was not a factor. Ireland was the most notable as in the run up to the crisis its national debt was well under 40 per cent. However its financial sector was in crisis having expanded to many times GDP and it had a rampant housing boom. Spain also had under 40 per cent of sovereign debt, but a huge private debt crisis related to housing and construction. Portugal, too, was close to the European average with similar levels to France and Germany. When these countries found their costs and levels of borrowing rocketing, the fact that their level of sovereign debt could be traced to banking and housing crashes and not government expenditure was overlooked.

In contrast to the claims of handbag economics, government debt was not a widespread problem in the leading economies prior to the crisis (except for Greece). As Steve Keen argues, the problem was private debt at record levels, with the position in 2008 much worse than in the 1930s as countries like the US had gone into recession at much higher levels (2009a: 3). Andreas Botsch cites European Commission evidence to show that private debt in Europe increased by more than 50 per cent between 1999 and 2007 while government debt to GDP ratios fell across the EU. After the crash there was a 'great rechristening' whereby the private debt crisis, caused by a 'deregulated financial sector gone mad', was re-labelled as a 'sovereign debt crisis' caused by 'profligate governments in Southern Europe' (Botsch 2013: 17). The result was that public, not private, debt became the primary policy focus. The problem shifted from the failures of commercial banking and capitalist finance to the profligacy of governments. TINA was back in the saddle once more and handbag economics tightened its grip even harder. The result was public sector austerity, a product of the 'dead ideas' of 'zombie economics' (Quiggin 2010) that seemed intent on killing the living.

Mark Blyth sees the Greek situation as providing the cloak behind which the 'Austerians' could rechristen private debt as public debt and then blame governments for the crisis of private finance (2013: 73). He sees the attack on public expenditure as ideological. Unlike the Keynesian approach that would raise and lower public expenditure in response to the rise and fall of the business cycle, Austerians only have one direction for public expenditure – down. Austerity programmes were also often accompanied by a change of government and the use of harsh political rhetoric. This was particularly true in the UK where the Conservative-Liberal Democrat coalition claimed the crisis was entirely the fault of the 1997–2010 Labour government. The Tory-led coalition reversed Labour's stimulus programme and announced its aim to move quickly towards a balanced budget, even a surplus, through the imposition of austerity.

The imposition of austerity can be seen as similar to the structural adjustment programmes imposed on countries that experienced financial problems in the wake of the so-called Third World debt crisis. In the Eurozone there was a similar problem of money from stronger economies flooding into weaker ones. Rather than blame being placed upon the risky lender, all blame was placed on the sovereign borrower. The solution was for indebted states to become more exposed to 'market forces' while shrinking the public sector. This leaves the question as to what was really being rescued, the indebted country or the banks that had made the 'toxic' loans? Greece's problems were as much a reflection of the unbalanced nature of European trade and finance as Greek government failures. As will be discussed in Chapter 7, within a monetary system there must not be a 'Minotaur', an economy that dominates production and does not reciprocate with consumption (Varoufakis 2011). The Eurozone has the historic problem of the dominance of Germany which accounts for 25 per cent of total output (Bivens 2013: 39). As European integration progressed, the southern states of the Eurozone saw a spectacular collapse in growth as they failed to compete on wages and prices. The limitations of the Eurozone as only a commercial currency union meant there was no institution at the centre to see fair play and redistribute resources as in a nation state. The single currency also meant that the usual responses of currency devaluation to make exchange rates more competitive were not available. Countries were therefore 'compelled to pursue internal devaluation via price and nominal wage deflation' (Botsch 2013: 9). This was compounded by the imposition of austerity following the crisis.

The justification of austerity was that the 'money markets' would not supply new debt to overburdened governments. This appeared reasonable since the bailout was required when states faced an escalation in the costs of borrowing on the financial market. However austerity was imposed even when there was no rise in borrowing costs as in the UK. Even for the bailout states, borrowing rates came down so that some could come out of their bailout status, that is, they were able to raise money on the open market again. What the advocates of handbag ideology failed to grasp was that for financial sector investors in the post-crisis period, state borrowing was seen as the safer option, particularly where states had their own currency like the US and the UK. While handbag economics aimed to shrink the state, hungry financial investors were avidly seeking new sovereign debt as the safest haven for their money. Central to their security was the public capacity in the short run to raise taxes and in the last resort to create public money. Even countries in the problem areas of Eurozone could attract low interest long-term loans.

Blyth argues that the push for austerity should be seen in an historical context. The attack on state spending is not just a feature of modern neoliberalism, but a product of classical liberalism. The state of that time was a ruling monarch who exercised the right to the assets of the realm in tax or kind. Classical liberalism was a political philosophy that represented a defence of private property and individual rights against the monarchy (Blyth 2013: 104). However, emerging capitalism also needed public authority. The emerging bourgeoisie needed services it wasn't willing to pay for: 'Thus the liberal dilemma that generates austerity is born. *The state: can't live with it, can't live without it, don't want to pay for it*' (Blyth 2013: 106, italics in original). The state spending that the classical liberals opposed was mainly for extravagance and war. Modern austerity is directed at the people and expenditure on universal public services, welfare, pensions, public infrastructure. The enemy here is not the monarch but the workers who could use their democratic power to sustain their livelihoods.

Democracy meant that politicians seeking re-election could be swayed by the masses to maintain current levels of expenditure by putting state activity in place of a collapsing market. The threat to neoliberal austerity is democracy itself as a challenge to the market (Blyth 2013: 178). The danger is that austerity will destroy democracy by driving the people to populist extremism.

Whereas Keynes would argue that the state needed to maintain employment while the market resurrected itself, neoliberal Austerians seek a bonfire of public services. Central to this is a debate about money. Supply-side neoliberals want money to accumulate privately as savings, in order to restart the cycle of investment. This requires increased inequality so that money can heap up for the wealthy while the workers become cheaper. For Keynes, the fallacy of this view was the assumption that heaped up money would automatically lead to investment. Instead it might be hoarded. As of 2015 the non-financial corporate sector is sitting on a mountain of cash and the banks are holding high levels of reserves, but the market is still on its knees.

Andreas Botsch has identified seven 'deadly hypocrisies' of neo-liberalism: that austerity can reduce debt; the confusion of public with private debt (the household analogy); the assumption that a public deficit/debt reduces growth (the Rogoff and Reinhart thesis); placing the blame on profligate governments (that only really applied to Greece with Goldman Sachs' help); that the EU is rescuing lazy southern states, rather than saving the financial bacon of northern European lenders and investors; the idea that austerity can drive competitiveness rather than a race to the bottom; that regulation alone will resolve the structural problems (Botsch 2013: 15).

Despite an early Keynesian response to the crisis, based on vast amounts of public money saving the banking sector from meltdown, neoliberal handbag economics won the day and austerity was imposed.

Crisis, Rescue, Punishment: From Keynesianism to Austerity

The crisis saw dramatic changes in the policy approach. It swept from outpourings of public resources to prevent the banking and financial sectors collapsing, to austerity for the people and small government, to mass infusions of public money once again through quantitative easing programmes for the financial sector. The latter ran alongside austerity programmes. It was cornucopia for the financial sector but privation for the people. In the early stages of the crisis there was a Keynesian response of large-scale public intervention. The US, in particular, has remained much more Keynesian throughout, despite the political difficulties with the Tea Party faction and Republican opposition to raising Federal borrowing levels. According to Wray, in the US 'The Fed spent (buying assets) and lent a total of $29 trillion to rescue the financial system' (2012: 89). While countries such as the UK and the US could quickly bring newly created public currency into play (albeit mostly designated as debt), countries that did not control their own currency were left to find the money where they could.

The initial widespread public response to the crisis made it seem as if handbag economics would be defeated. The financial sector was in disgrace and the centrality of public finance to its survival was plain to see. However, that window of opportunity for change was lost. Social and political movements who might have been in a position to present an alternative monetary and financial strategy, had none. Certainly there were spirited protest movements such as Occupy, but no proposals that could challenge TINA. Left groups had an analysis of a crisis between labour and capital, and a critique of finance capital, but virtually nothing to say on the problem of public money supply in financialised and privatised monetary systems. Certainly there were voices in the wings, many of whom will be discussed in this book, but they had yet to find an activist audience.

Because there was no mainstream political or academic base to support the early public action in response to the 2007–8 crisis, the bank bailouts were turned against the public sector. Rather than the banking crisis being seen as the problem, the pressure focused upon what was seen as unpayable sovereign debt. The answer was to reduce public expenditure through austerity measures until the debt came back to 'acceptable' levels. The brick wall of neoliberal ideology, and the failure of alternative thinking to make headway, meant that the Keynesian window closed sharply, helped by three factors.

The first propaganda coup for handbag economics was the collapse of Greek public finances in 2010. As discussed above, Greece was the first European country to need a bailout and the only one whose problems with unmanageable sovereign debt could be clearly traced to problems in government finances rather than a banking crisis. Handbag economics got a second huge boost in 2010 with the publication of an academic paper that seemed to prove that government debt above 90 per cent of GDP led to a fall in growth (Reinhart and Rogoff 2010). Although the statistical evidence underpinning this finding was later found to be faulty, the damage had been done, and widespread austerity programmes were implemented (Herndon, Ash and Pollin 2013). A third boost to handbag economics came from another academic paper that argued that public austerity was a good thing for economies. In a kind of scorched earth approach, 'expansionary fiscal contraction' argued that a bonfire of the public sector would lead to a phoenix-like resurrection of the private sector (Alesina and Ardagna 2010). Paul Krugman described this approach as being equivalent to believing in the 'confidence fairy' (2012: 195). Unfortunately the adoption of austerity to conjure up the confidence fairy remained central to British and European economic policy, somewhat less so in the US.

As one commentator puts it, 'Looking through ideology and rhetoric, it is hard not to conclude that European policy responses since the beginning of the crisis, and particularly since 2010, have had the paramount goal of preserving the stability of the European banking system as an end in itself, with little thought as to what that would mean in terms of short and medium term macroeconomic outcomes' (Silvers 2013: 100). While substantial injections of public money had relieved the pressure on European banks, there was no relief for the debt-ridden public, whether individuals or states. By 2011 Mario Draghi, head of the European Central Bank, had pumped a trillion euros into European banks through cheap loans, although most of the money was left in ECB reserves as banks still refused to increase lending. By July 2012 Draghi was forced to say 'The ECB is ready to do whatever it takes to preserve the euro', and in September 2012 he announced 'outright monetary transactions', that is, not just providing cheap money to banks, but buying up bonds directly. By late 2014 he was cutting interest rates to 0.05 per cent and charging banks 0.1 per cent to leave their money in central bank reserves. This did little good as the Eurozone still faced deflation, a potentially unstoppable collapse in prices. In Japan, Abenomics also faced the same problem of trying to flood the financial sector with money. As Keynes remarked many years ago, trying to get people to borrow or lend when they don't want to is like pushing on a string. It remains to be seen how successful the Eurozone quantitative easing programme will be.

The focus was also upon rescuing the financial sector, rather than looking at the position of households. As Silvers points out, in the US total outlays to banks in terms of equity and subsidised debt was measured in the trillions, whereas total assistance to households in the TARP (Troubled Asset Relief Programme) was approximately $50 billion, most of which has been unspent. This differed from the Great Depression and the Savings and Loan Crisis, where there was a write down of inflated bank assets and relief to bank borrowers (Silvers 2013: 100). Despite this harsh approach, there is no evidence that austerity works. In the 1930s, only when austerity was abandoned did things improve (Blyth 2013: 179). Nor is there evidence of reform of the banking and financial sector. The main public policy solution appears to be getting the financial sector back into the saddle with some small regulatory features such as a tax on financial transactions (the Tobin tax) and some proposals for separating bank functions that remain to be implemented. In the UK the relatively mild recommendations of a commission on banking were kicked a long way down the road under pressure from the banks.

Despite the massive public rescue, neoliberalism seemed to have lost none of its force. Even as states were pouring public money into the privatised financial sector, they were condemned as undermining market forces. Public assets were stripped and public services curtailed. Unemployment rose and civic unrest threatened. A major reason for the ideological hegemony of neoliberalism was the marginalisation of critical voices as neoclassical and handbag economics had closed down academic debate for more than three decades.

The Eclipse of Pluralism in Economics: TINA's Academic Bag-carriers

In the decades before the 2007–8 crisis the economics profession had become an academic monoculture dominated by neoclassical theory. Orthodox economics sought to demonstrate its credentials as a science through the use of extensive mathematical modelling with an emphasis on individualised utility maximisation, rational choice and the tendency to equilibrium. Heterodox economists, in contrast, derived their methodology from the social sciences and focused on actual behaviour and institutions (Lee 2012). The dominance of orthodoxy saw Keynesianism, political economy and issues such as ethics sidelined in economics teaching and research. Orthodox gate-keepers closed off access to academic jobs and academic publishing driving other economic perspectives out of universities and excluding them from key publications. In July 2014 a report from the Association Français D'Economie Politique (AFEP) (French Association of Political Economy) showed how the criteria for evaluating research, and the competitive examination for recruitment to Higher Education teaching in France, favoured orthodox approaches. They found that only 5 per cent of recruits to university posts between 2005–11 could be described as pluralists. If this bias continues, as the remaining heterodox professors leave or retire and are replaced by mainstream appointees, pluralism in economics teaching could be totally eliminated in the next five to eight years.

Market fundamentalist neoclassical views continued to dominate economic theory despite major crises in 1992, 1987–8, 1998, 2000 and particularly the crisis of 2007–8. Rather than facing the challenge, 'toxic finance and toxic economic theorising became mutually reinforcing processes' (Varoufakis 2011: 14, italics in the original). One reason that Europe's policymakers have pursued neoliberal policies is that many of the staff of the European Central Bank (ECB) and European finance ministries have been trained in Chicago school neoliberal economics (Palley 2013a:12). The economics profession's adoption of the dominant neoclassical paradigm can be seen in terms of Kuhn's (1962) model of a 'normal science' paradigm that rejects all alternative views, although it was not without its challengers (Lawson 1997, Keen 2011, Chang 2014).

Neoclassical economic modelling allowed its theories to be untainted by the inconvenience of real people in their real lives. As crisis followed crisis, economics students protested against the narrow confines of the subject as defined by the dominant paradigm. Following the 2000 dot-com debacle a campaign was launched by economics students in France for pluralism that had resonance in many other countries. Following the 2008 crisis students once again demanded change. By May 2014, 65 student organisations from 30 countries had come together to demand changes to economics curricula arguing that the current monoculture could not address major issues such as financial instability, food security and climate change. An open letter called for pluralism at three levels, theoretical, methodological and inter-disciplinary (www.isipe.net). Students were also organising their own lectures with invited speakers from different schools of thought. If Kuhn is correct, the dominant paradigm cannot continue indefinitely against disconfirming evidence. There is a wealth of material in print and online that presents clear alternatives. Hopefully this book will add to that critical mass and alternative paradigm(s) will eventually prevail. The best-selling status of books by Thomas Piketty and Ha-Joon Chang is a good sign.

The dominance of neoclassical economics was a major defeat for Keynesianism as the main economic approach of the early to mid-twentieth century. Writing in the shadow of the Great Depression, Keynes' aim to achieve a shared prosperity resonated with the postwar generation and the role of government in the economy was not questioned. In Britain the postwar Labour government introduced major programmes of welfare provision and nationalisation of key sectors of the economy including the Bank of England. Despite both government debt and deficit being very high at the time, postwar growth saw these falling rapidly and the 1950s are often seen as a golden era of a mixed economy in which the European Model of economic partnership between labour and capital was developed. Given the excesses that led to the Great Depression the role of finance was clearly defined. In the US under New Deal regulation the role of finance was to (1) provide business and entrepreneurs with finance for investment; (2) provide households with mortgage finance for home acquisition; (3) provide business and households with insurance services; (4) provide households with saving instruments to meet future needs; and (5) provide business and households with transactions services (Palley 2013b: 73). These restrictions and responsibilities peeled away as the financial sector broke free and captured not only the money supply but the theoretical high ground.

Privatised Money and Public Responsibility:
The Contradiction of a Debt-based Money Supply

The postwar compromise broke down as money and finance escaped from public control and growing prosperity faltered in the face of stagflation in the 1970s. Neoliberalism saw the problem of low growth as lying with an inflexible and powerful labour force and too large a state. Monetarism saw inflation as caused by there being too much money in circulation. Neither solution succeeded. Destroying the trades unions and attempting to limit the welfare state have not solved the imbalances in global capitalism. The monetarist experiment failed because it proved impossible to monitor the rapidly privatising money supply or control it with the instruments central banks had to hand, mainly interest rates. The sharp rise in interest rates did, however, cause major problems for indebted developing countries.

One thing that monetarism did reveal was that the power of state monetary authorities was limited, as the privatisation of the money supply took hold. As Konings has argued, the financial crisis was not a failure of public policy but a systemic crisis within a privatised financial system: 'the current crisis is not a product of politics and regulation having let the market spin out of control, but precisely a product of contradictions internal to the operation of power and control, of financial power having gone beyond its own conditions of possibility' (2009: 123). The ideological justification for privatised control of the creation and circulation of money as debt was that it put economic responsibility on to the borrower. This was compared with the possibility of creating public money free of debt, derided as 'printing money'. Privately created money on the other hand was being 'paid for' by borrowers agreeing to repayment with interest. It was assumed that people, companies and governments would not borrow what they could not repay, nor would lenders lend to those whose creditworthiness was in doubt. What was ignored was the likelihood of major risk and, in particular, systemic risk. Risk was also profitable, which meant that those who took the greatest risks made the most profit and thereby determined the direction of the economy. However the biggest problem was that an unsustainable financial order was gambling with public money.

The main flaw of handbag economics lies in the privatisation of the supply of public currency into the supply of credit, that is, debt. Tying money supply to debt means that if debt dries up or becomes unsustainable so does the money supply. This is a problem not just for the market, but for society as a whole. For the market, the failure of credit supply threatens economic breakdown, but so too does the loss of the supply of public money. Public money, the trusted public currency, is needed to authorise trades and accumulate profit. As many commentators have argued, debt cannot be the basis of money supply because a debt-based system is always subject to crisis, to boom and bust. There is no such thing as stability, as Minsky pointed out, it just leads to complacency and increased risk.

While the public has lost control of the supply of their public currency, they have not shed their liability for it. Although the 'public as household' is denied the right to create money on its own account, the modern privatised money machine is creating money designated as public currency. This was not always the case. Private banks did create private money (notes and accounts of various kinds), while states jealously guarded the right to create or control coin. However, as commercial banking developed, public and private money became more integrated, as will be discussed in Chapters 4 and 5. In modern fiat money systems, the distinction has completely broken down. Banks only issue bank notes drawn on the central bank and states and banks both work through accounts recorded in the public currency. Modern banks are not creating private money. They are not creating loans in 'Lloyds florins' or 'HSBC guineas'. They are creating bank accounts that represent the public currency (pounds, dollars). Because of the history of state money and bank private lending, the view prevails in the literature that banks are creating an inferior 'credit money', leaving the state to create 'money proper' or 'high powered money'. This distinction implies different types of public currency: 'real money' (cash and central bank reserves) as against inferior bank account records. In modern monetary systems this distinction is no longer viable (if it ever was).

As the experience of bank crashes shows, people do not see their bank accounts as not 'real money'. Neither does the state rescue banks with piles of notes and coins. State money is as intangible as bank money. The distinction between the two sorts of money is not a difference in essence but a difference in provenance. Whereas bank-created money is only created as debt, public money can be created free of debt. Both create new currency that must be honoured by the public in whose name the money is created. As will be explained more fully in Chapter 4, bank lending is not based on a transfer of depositors' savings of 'real money'; it creates new public currency. This new debt-based public currency has then to be 'backed' by public monetary authorities, usually the central bank. However, the central bank only backs the transferability of the money, its social and public trust as legal tender. The purchasing power of that money is backed by the labour, goods and resources of people living within the monetary community.

A major contradiction of tying money supply to debt is that the creator of the money always wants more money back than they have issued. Debt-based money must be continually repaid with interest. As money is continually being repaid, new debt must be being generated if the money supply is to be maintained. Just as the debt-based money supply rapidly expands in times of optimism, when that falters it will quickly go into reverse as new debt is not taken out and old debt is still being repaid. The demand for interest also means that at any point in time the creator of the money supply is owed more money than they have issued in aggregate. This builds a growth dynamic into the money supply that would frustrate the aims of those who seek to achieve a more socially and ecologically sustainable economy. It also means that a large number of people are in debt peonage, forced to labour to repay mortgage, consumer, personal or student debt. As debt is central to the production and circulation of commodities, all consumers are paying the interest on commercial debt, as the late German campaigner Margrit Kennedy pointed out.

The commodification of the public currency supply as debt also raises the question of its moral basis. Historically many societies have expressed concern at the existence of debt and particularly interest, especially where this is compounded so that interest becomes payable on interest. The problem of extortionate levels of interest as well as unpayable debt led to rules about usury and the need for periodic jubilee debt redemptions (Graeber 2011). Concern about the balance of power between lender and borrowers is still embodied in Islamic principles of banking where the creditor shares the risk (and benefit) with the borrower. Debt then becomes much closer to equity. From an ecological perspective there is also the concern that the need to repay debt with interest drives economic growth with a detrimental impact on people and planet.

The dominant neoliberal paradigm is deeply flawed. It sees the public sector as equivalent to a dependent household while being deeply dependent upon it for rescue when in crisis. In modern bank-led money systems the public is taking responsibility for the integrity of its public currency, while the private sector retains control and the financial benefit. The immense level of state resources made available in the bank bailout and the central role of the state in securing money systems has re-established the role of states as monetary agents. What became clear as the financial crisis unfolded was that the financial sector could not be seen as independent. Given that the privatised money supply system relies on explicit and implicit public guarantees, Martin Wolf of the UK *Financial Times* argues that the commercial banking system is not in the private sector at all. It is more like an uncontrolled civil service (2014: 198).

Although deposit account guarantees are capped (in Europe to the equivalent of 100,000 euros), in practice, states such as Ireland have had to underpin their whole financial sector. The lesson of Lehman Brothers was that in finance and banking everything is connected to everything else. Global financial institutions were entangled with each other and with state monetary systems. Despite the need for central banks to 'back' commercial bank lending, neoliberal policies demand that central banks should be 'independent', that is, not subject to democratic control. As a result, central banks became almost entirely focused on serving the interests of the banking and financial sector. This was particularly the case for the European Central Bank which had no framework for representing the public interest. As will be discussed further in Chapter 5, central banks in financialised economies have largely lost their 'public' face of public money creation for public or sovereign benefit.

The privatisation of the public money supply as debt is based on the assumption that competition for money enables its best use.

Profit-driven markets are seen as the best mechanism to provide the goods and services people need. Market exchange for money is the mechanism by which the hidden hand of personal greed magically turns into the capacity to meet the demands and desires of the people. However this does not meet the needs of all the people, or take account of the social and environmental costs. It leads to a harsh world where people who cannot labour for wages or obtain debt are left without the means of sustaining themselves. They are seen as a drain on the rest of society, dependent on welfare. Welfare is seen as a charity rather than a right, despite the fact that in the UK the welfare budget also supports the working poor. It is an economy without compassion. Through the ideology of handbag economics, austerity is imposed to save the future of capitalism by sacrificing the people.

While there was quantitative easing for the banks, there was none for the people as austerity threatened to cause social breakdown. Publicly provided goods and services are not seen as a benefit to the people, a source of public wealth, because they are not traded for private profit. For capitalism, wealth is defined as the accumulation of assets that can be realised in money form or invested to produce more accumulated assets in the future. Wealth is not considered in terms of public benefit, social solidarity, personal flourishing, the preservation of the natural world, or peace of mind that each individual will receive the care they need in the cycle of life.

The choice between debt and democracy is between a money system based on privatised debt and the debt-free public creation and circulation of the public currency. Handbag economics has no monetary role for the public as represented by the public sector. People only appear as borrowers, consumers and taxpayers. Who accesses the public currency and how they use it is a private matter on which the public as citizens have no right to comment. The possibility of public control of money creation is dismissed as 'printing money' despite the fact that banks are continually adding new numbers to bank accounts, which amounts to the same thing. As Botsch argues: 'Making finance serve society and the real economy necessitates a financial sector that is smaller in size, slower in speed, simpler in structure, separated functionally, less short-term oriented and, not least, democratized' (2013: 21).

As will be argued in the next chapter, an ecologically sustainable, sufficiency provisioning system cannot be built on a debt-based monetary system. There are many other ways in which socially just and ecologically sustainable provisioning systems have been organised that have lessons for the democratisation of public money.

2

Money for Sustainability, Sufficiency and Social Justice

After a crisis such as that of 2007–8 and the ensuing imposition of austerity measures, the desire to return as quickly as possible to business as usual is understandable. However, a crisis creates the opportunity to raise fundamental questions about the direction that contemporary economies are taking. The problem of ecological sustainability has long been on the political agenda, with the threat of climate change widely recognised. However, the radical *economic* change necessary to achieve a reduction in ecological damage is not being addressed by the mainstream. Although conventional economics is framed in terms of scarcity and competition for the most efficient use of resources, scarcity is seen as relative to the presumed unlimited nature of human desire rather than the limit of the resources themselves. The idea of unlimited desire does not allow for the possibility that people would be satisfied with a lower level of consumption, that is, for the notion of sufficiency.

Sufficiency can be defined as the principle of enough (Skidelsky and Skidelsky 2012, Dietz and O'Neill, 2013). Enough in ecological terms is different from enough in socioeconomic terms. Although there are debates about where the limits lie, there are ecological boundaries to particular kinds of growth. Most planetary resources are finite. Failure to recognise this leads to a global corporate economy based on the promise of unlimited growth that has become 'a permanent war economy against the planet and people' (Shiva 2012: 3). The socio-economic notion of 'enough' is comparative rather than absolute. It is what lies between not enough and too much. It is a concept that necessarily entails equality; sufficiency for one must be sufficiency

46

for all, otherwise some will have more than sufficient and others will have less.

Even if the claim that human desire is unlimited is true, the market solution tackles the problem of scarcity from the wrong end. It assumes a given level of resources for which people compete. This does not address the need to limit desire itself. Competition for limited resources also implies exclusion and inequality. The strongest, richest and most resourceful must win. There is no possibility of resources being shared. Such ethical questions are avoided by assuming that the limits are not in the resources themselves, but in the greed of the competitors. Actual scarcity raises the question of the allocation of scarce resources and the principles of equality and socioeconomic justice. Rather than amoral competition this would imply the ethical case for a right to livelihood, not just for humans but for all life forms, and the need to sustain inanimate resources.

Ownership and control of natural resources is, or should be, central to both green and socialist thought. While socialists have stressed public ownership and control of the means of production, this also needs to embrace common ownership of the means of sustenance. Equally, green approaches need to explore ownership as well as conservation. Commitment to common ownership is often expressed in terms of re-establishing the commons either as nature in its own right or as a socially managed resource. Comparisons are often drawn with the historical enclosure of common land. For Martin Large, modern corporate economies represent 'an age of enclosure, of privatisation (of) our commons – whether gifts of nature such as land, water, air, seeds, the human genome or commons resulting from human creativity such as capital, the financial system, public assets, culture, health, education – have been made into commodities for sale on the market' (2010: 5). He sees the banks as having 'plundered our financial commons' in a market fundamentalist free for all. In contrast, Large promotes the idea of a commonwealth which prioritises equality and mutuality. For Vandana Shiva, recovering the commons is essential to establishing the '"Enoughness" that would be necessary to achieve both peace and freedom' (2012: 262). Rupert Read hopes that 'commons-sense' will eventually become 'commonsense'. He sees this as an 'ancient future' where the search for profit and accumulation would be replaced by 'a return to living in and on the commons' (2014: 189).

From these perspectives that stress ecological sustainability, sufficiency and the importance of re-establishing the commons, the aim in response to the 2007–8 crisis would be to move from the imposition of austerity to a socially just and ecologically sustainable sufficiency commons-based provisioning system. Provisioning is used here as a wider concept than economy, which is mainly associated with the market (Power 2004, Mellor 2010a, 2010b). The concept of provisioning cannot be limited to what is provided by profit-driven markets or publicly funded expenditure. Provisioning must embrace needs that are currently spread across the spectrum of market, public and social provision. Provisioning includes unpaid work and the work of nature in providing resources and replenishment that contribute to human well-being. As they are based on debt and the search for profit-driven growth, capitalist markets and the privatised money system of neoliberal handbag economics cannot achieve ecological sustainability, sufficiency provisioning or social justice. Nor could they (re)establish the commons or commonwealth. A commons-based, ecologically sustainable and socially just system of provisioning must be democratic and based primarily on debt-free public or social money.

Privatised Money and Ecological Unsustainability

One of the earliest thinkers to directly link ecological destructiveness with the monetary system of market economics was the British Nobel Laureate Frederick Soddy (1926). He drew a distinction between real wealth, that is, the wealth of the environment, and virtual wealth, that is, money and money value. He was particularly concerned about debt. He pointed out that natural systems were limited and prone to an increase in entropy, moving from usable to unusable states. Debts, on the other hand, grow exponentially. The incompatibility of natural systems and money systems has been similarly argued for by Herman Daly (1999) who called for reform of the monetary system to enable a move towards a steady state economy that reflects the capacity of nature to absorb human activity without degradation. The most fundamental demand of green economics is that economies should live within their ecological means, that is, their use of resources should be compatible with the ecological dynamics of the planet (Georgescu-Roegen 1971, Herman Daly 1973). Approaches to economics need to take account of environmental constraints (Panayotakis 2011). This may require not only a halt to growth but even degrowth in some contexts (Latouche 2009).

A major driver of growth is the debt-based nature of modern money systems. The level of personal debt and financial leverage in the build up to the crisis reflected the fact that debt had become the main way money was supplied in many contemporary economies. The constant need to repay debts with interest creates an unsustainable growth dynamic (Douthwaite 2000, Cato 2009). Debt affects the ability of households to lower their economic footprint by cutting their income. When Keynes predicted that by the end of the twentieth century people would only be working 15 hours a week, he did not foresee falling wages and escalating debt.

The commodification of value in market economies has also been criticised for externalising the ecosystem by failing to take account of the cost of the destruction of the natural environment. Monetary value only reflects what is bought and sold for profit. If prices do not reflect the real cost of ecological damage or the use of 'free' resources such as clean air and water, there is the danger they will be abused. One solution has been the attempt to put a market price on environmental values. However inequality means that the price has to be very high to stop higher earners consuming, while those on lower incomes suffer from lack of access to necessary resources. It is also difficult to artificially set a market price or predict market conditions, as the failure of carbon trading has shown. The inadequacy of market solutions has led to more radical proposals. Ideas have been put forward to bring down energy use, such as contraction and convergence, where all economies contract towards a sustainable level and converge on a principle of equal usage of natural resources, or cap and share, where a 'capped' supply of pollution or resource use permits are sold by global public authorities and the income generated is made available to poorer communities and economies rather than being left to market forces as it is in carbon trading (Cato 2009: 111).

Far from supporting the assertion that business can address ecological sustainability (Cohen 2011), a report on the possibilities for green growth and environmental resilience in Asia and the Pacific shows the limits of private finance. Arguing that economies need to be recalibrated to address environmental sustainability if they are to achieve a 'better quality of economic growth', the report anticipates that lack of private sector funding may prove a stumbling block (United Nations and Asian Development Bank 2012: xix). While the report hopes that finance will come from the market, with green growth as a market leader, finance for such initiatives is a particular problem because of the high initial cost of more sustainable approaches with any benefit being recouped over the long term. The report calls for 'specific and complementary financing mechanisms' to close the 'time gap' (2012: 102). What this means is public funding through a combination of loans, equity investment, guarantees and grants. Once again, public funds will be necessary before the market can function. Some countries have worked out the cost of detailed Green New Deal plans, such as South Korea which proposed expenditure of $36,280 million creating 960,000 jobs (Barbier 2010: 176).

However, the problem of public funding in a privatised money system still remains. While states spent huge amounts of money to meet the financial crisis, there is no indication that they are willing to put such a level of funds into the ecological crisis. As Tim Jackson has argued, it is 'delusional' to assume that it will be possible to stabilise the climate and protect against resource scarcity through capitalism's presumed 'propensity for efficiency' (2009: 7). What kind of money system could support a sufficiency green economy? As Richard Douthwaite has argued, 'sustainability requires a money supply system that can run satisfactorily if growth stops' (1999: 27). This, and the wider question of what kind of alternative economics and politics is possible, has been addressed from a range of green and social justice perspectives (Barry 2012, Robertson 2012, Nadal 2011, Hahnel 2011, Barbier 2010, Boyle and Simms 2009).

David Boyle and Andrew Simms call for a 'new economics' that will deal with the triple crises of credit, climate change and energy (2009: 3). Proposals for a Green New Deal echo Roosevelt's New Deal following the 1930s Depression. In 2008 the UK's New Economics Foundation's version of a Green New Deal called for government-led investment in energy efficiency and innovations such as micro-generation of power, green jobs and low carbon infrastructure, a windfall tax on the profits of oil and gas companies, financial incentives for green investment and reduced energy usage, re-regulated green banking based on smaller banks, capital controls to stop destabilising capital flows, prevention of speculative profits such as derivatives, and a clampdown on tax evasion, tax avoidance and tax havens (Green New Deal Group 2008, Boyle and Simms 2009: 157–8).

Sufficiency and Social Justice

A sufficiency green economy would aim to provide enough goods and services to enable each person to flourish without causing ecological damage. The aim would be to remove the impetus for environmentally damaging growth and create the potential for socially just degrowth where necessary. For Panayotakis, a sufficiency economy must be based on principles of social justice and democracy: 'only a society based on economic democracy can manage scarcity in a radical and humane fashion' (2011: 6). Economic democracy would also mean ensuring that economic priorities were determined in the interests of the most vulnerable members of the community (Hutchinson, Mellor and Olsen 2002: 209). Sufficiency provisioning must also enable people to experience livelihood security, knowing that enough will be available.

Destructive growth in the present system is driven by its structure as a 'two-step' economy. To obtain what they need people must work in areas that are deemed commercially profitable, even if they have no personal need of the goods or services produced. Social and public provision depends on some of the income or profit from commercial activities being transferred. Sufficiency provisioning would need to be based on a one-step relationship between work and consumption where people mainly work in activities that are related to their needs. There is a long history in green economics of challenging the nature of work in contemporary economies (Cato 2009: 55–68). Work in a debt-based economy can have social and ecological implications if people have to work unnecessarily hard or long, or engage in ecologically destructive patterns of production in order to repay their debts. Campaigners for alternative approaches to work have long called for it to be under personal control (Robertson 1985), be useful (Illich 1977), and be part of an economics 'as if people mattered' (Schumacher 1973). Local money systems and other green alternatives are seen as enabling a more balanced lifestyle. Debt-based and prof-it-driven market systems mean that people can only have influence at the 'end of pipe', the point of purchase. Decisions about production and investment lie with those who can harness money and finance. If the aim of a sufficiency economy is to move towards a one-step integration of work and needs, the public must be involved at the 'start of pipe' where priorities are set.

Democratisation of how priorities are determined for investment would open a debate about how money is allocated and used. At present, investment decisions are considered to be a private matter as individuals or companies are accessing 'private' credit. However, as has been argued in the previous chapter, if that 'private credit' involves the creation of public currency, the public has a right to be consulted. Would a financial system under democratic control have favoured such huge amounts of bank-created money being poured into the financial sector without any accompanying controls or demands? From both a green and social justice perspective, resource scarcity demands much more active public participation in the economic process. For Panayotakis, 'economic democracy (is) the condition for the use of scarce resources that is consistent with ecological sustainability, the elimination of unnecessary human suffering, and a richer life for all human beings on this planet' (2011: 149). As Boyle and Simms argue, a green economy would operate on very different principles. Corporations would need to be 'legally accountable to society at large ... structured in such a way that their prime purpose is to tackle the basic problems of humanity'. This would require 'reorganizing the way we measure success so that ... decisions are based on human well-being rather than the false progress of fluctuating money growth' (2009: 158).

Sufficiency can only be defined in real terms, that is, the actual provisioning of needs. In mainstream economics there is no distinction between needs and wants, both are captured in the notion of desired consumption. Sufficiency provisioning cannot avoid addressing the priorities of needs versus wants. Seeing money as representing consumer demand individualises those priorities into consumer choice, as against more social and public debates about collective provisioning. As Lee argues, mainstream economics has 'no substantive meaning or explanatory power regarding the social provisioning process' (2012: 339). To enable these debates to be socially and publicly meaningful the role of money needs to be discussed at the point of creation and allocation, not at the level of individualised employment or consumption. The market is also not a helpful focus for decision-making because of the externalities involved. As discussed earlier, much of the use of, and damage to, the environment is not costed into monetary accounts. The same is true of much unpaid community and domestic work, which would be embraced by the wider concept of provisioning.

There is a danger that critiques of the financial sector are limited to a concern with its impact on the 'real economy', taken to mean the productive aspects of the market economy. This does not address provisioning that embraces the whole of people's lives and the life of nature. The 'real economy' of sufficiency provisioning cannot be limited to productive work, it must address the embodiedness of humans' existence as organic beings, that is, be framed by humans' embeddedness in nature. This broader conception of human provisioning brings together the work of nature with work surrounding the human body, and opens up the question of the gendered nature of economic systems.

The Externalisation of Women's Work and Nature's Resources

Both greens and feminists have argued that market economies do not take account of the 'work' of women and of nature. The externalised aspects of human embodiment (women's work) and human embeddedness (relying on the sustainability of the natural environment) are both treated as a free good. As a result, the benefits of women's unpaid work, like the cost of damage to the natural environment, are not acknowledged. Ecofeminist political economy has brought these critiques together to argue that the gendered nature of modern economies leads to their ecological destructiveness because they have been constructed on a false basis that excludes much of the materiality of human lives (Mellor 2013, 1997). The inconveniences of humans' existence as natural beings are excluded from the framework of economic value as low-paid or unpaid 'women's work' (that may be done by men, but is more generally done by women). Economies are built around an artificial construct 'economic man' (who may be a woman, but is more generally male). Unsustainable economies are constructed by dominant men (and some women) in the interests of dominant men (and some women). The boundary that separates 'economic man' from 'women's work' is monetary value. This is reflected in both the public and market economies. Priorities for public expenditure reflect dominant interests and employment structures represent gender bias with women mainly in low-paid jobs.

Ecofeminists argue that the notion of an economy as representing activities defined by money value fails to acknowledge its true resource base and the way it is parasitical upon sustaining systems of unpaid social labour and the natural world (Mies 1998, Salleh 2009, Mellor 2009). As a result, these are exploited and damaged. The money-framed economy can operate as it does because it can exploit the unpaid, or underpaid, caring work that is mainly done by women, together with the resources of the natural world. Ecological sustainability would mean recognising the material structures that enable the false construct 'economic man' to seemingly transcend 'his' material conditions. A provisioning economy would start from a commitment to human well-being and the sustainability of the natural world. Patterns of work and consumption would be sensitive to the human life cycle and the replenishing needs of the planet. Provisioning of necessary goods and services would be the main focus of the economy and the activities of production and exchange would be fully integrated with the dynamics of the body and the environment.

To achieve provisioning sufficiency within ecological limits, a challenge needs to be made to the conception of value as price on the market. Rather than market value, account should be taken of what Ariel Salleh calls 'metabolic value'. Salleh sees capitalism as owing a 'debt' at three levels: social debt to exploited labour, embodied debt to reproductive labour, and ecological debt for damage to the natural metabolism (2009: 24). She points out that what she describes as eco-sufficiency is already to be found among the legions of 'meta-industrial' workers, 'indigenous, peasant and care-giving workers', that underpin the formal economy (2009: 291). A similar point is made by Biesecker and Hofmeister who argue that it is vital to look at the processes of mediation between society and nature, in particular the work of (re)productivity that would recognise that 'the processes involved in the regeneration and restoration of human and nonhuman life are intrinsic to each and every process involving the production of goods and services' (2010: 1707).

These 'processes of mediation' will not cease in a degrowth, sufficiency society. Rather they will become more difficult if lower energy use removes labour-saving domestic technology. If women are not to become overburdened, men will need to share this work which is repetitive and relentless. People must be fed, cleaned and cared for day in and day out. In his exploration of a degrowth 'concrete utopia', Latouche wants people to be weaned from commitment to 'the job' and instead rediscover 'the repressed dimensions of life: the leisure to do one's duty as a citizen, the pleasure of the freedom to engage in freely chosen arts and crafts activities, the sensation of having found time to play, contemplate, meditate, enjoy conversations or quite simply to enjoy being alive' (2009: 40–1). This is an attractive vision of a future life, but where is women's work? Where in this vision is the work of the body, feeding and hygiene, hand weeding and planting, animal husbandry, care for the young, old and sick? It is important to acknowledge that in a degrowth society there may be a conflict between women's desires to be liberated from the burdens of paid and unpaid work related to human needs, and the strategies for growth reduction and ecological sustainability.

The danger is that sufficient, sustainable provisioning will still be gendered. Localism is a prevalent theme in the degrowth approach, but if this is seen as a scaled-down version of the market, even with co-operative patterns of ownership, what will happen to more collective public provisioning? Women rely heavily on the provision of public services, and women do most of the nursing, hygiene, childcare and elderly care involved. What type of public provisioning would a degrowth system envisage? Tim Jackson agrees that a green economy would need to be 'ecologically and socially literate, ending the folly of separating economy from society and environment' (2009: 10). Failure to be literate with regard to gender may have negative consequences for women. For example, evidence from Costa Rica indicates that women are being adversely affected by the Kyoto protocol as they are driven from rainforest areas designated as carbon sinks (Isla 2009). The result is that many are now working in the sex industry. While it is obviously desirable 'to build a society in which we can live better lives by working less and consuming less' (Latouche 2009: 9), the gendered nature of modern economies must also be addressed, if the impact on women is not to be ignored.

Ecofeminist political economy adds to Marxian political economy the importance of gender in exploring the interaction of humanity with nature and critiquing the current structure of human provisioning. In doing so, it challenges the boundary of 'the economy' as defined by capitalism, and the role of money in defining that boundary. The analysis of class exploitation in production has not tended to pay attention to money as a phenomenon in its own right. However, from the perspective of women's unpaid work in reproduction, the role of money is important in separating off human activities that are not accorded commercial value or recognised in public accounts (Waring 1989). The question then arises, is the correct approach to attempt to democratise and generalise the use of money as advocated in this book, or should money be removed altogether?

Life Without Money

The case against money is that the desire and need for it distorts our relationships with each other and with the natural environment. The function of money as a medium of exchange and a measure of value is seen as synonymous with purely market values, while values that emphasise the quality of life and work are marginalised. From within ecofeminism, Veronika Bennholdt-Thomsen and Maria Mies (1999) have made the case for promoting and maintaining subsistence economies, claiming that market economies are alienated from the reality of human existence within the natural world. What is needed is a more human-scale approach to provisioning. From the perspective of non-market socialism, Anitra Nelson and Frans Timmerman (2011) advocate a money-free, market-free, class-free and state-free society. They see money as the main agent of capitalism; its structures, relations and values drive inequality and exploitation. Working within the framework of money, as in fair trade, ethical investment or carbon trading, they argue, is a delusion as it does not escape capitalist markets. Rejecting money is a route to the rejection of the whole panoply of capitalism, opening the way to collective sufficiency and ecological sustainability.

The political aim is to find money-free spaces. Bennholdt-Thomsen and Mies advocate preserving traditional peasant self-production as well as developing new forms of subsistence provisioning. Nelson and Timmerman advocate collective production through 'sharing economies' where people collectively plan, produce, share and care for one another. The benefit of more locally focused production is seen as empowering through shared knowledge and active participation. For Nelson and Timmerman, instead of a money system based on trade and contracts, there would be compacts and networks building up from the local level, linking the household, the neighbourhood and the bioregion. Expressed needs from the household up would be aggregated and negotiated through mechanisms of deliberative democracy. Deliberative democracy sees citizens as more than mere voters: they are actively involved in deliberation prior to decision-making (Dryzek 2010). The most important aim is to reject commodification and exchange value in favour of prioritising use value.

However, rejection of the *commercial* use of money need not imply rejection of the use of money *per se*. What the critics of money are rejecting is commodification through monetary exchange, the defining feature of capitalism. Rather than seeing the use of money as responsible for capitalist structures and values, capitalism can be seen as harnessing what is essentially a social and public construct, through the privatisation of money. This stance would lead to the need to reclaim and democratise money rather than abolish it. In the same way as changing the concept of 'economy' to that of 'provisioning' opens up new ways of addressing livelihood, the meaning of 'money' must be challenged. Historical and contemporary evidence shows that money can exist in social, public and commercial forms and varied modes of operation. It is necessary to rescue the social and public aspects of money from the dominance of market hegemony. This wider conception of money is not incompatible with the recognition of use value. Provisioning based on use value in a non-money system as set out by Nelson and Timmerman seems rather complex and unwieldy. The fact that most societies through history have had some form of money indicates that it is socially useful. Also, the practicality of provisioning large-scale societies with no money or only local money is questionable. Reasserting the role of public money and recognising the value of experiments in creating social money is arguably a more practical way forward. This requires an exploration of the nature of money.

Varieties of Money

Approaches to money depend on the theory of money adopted. As will be discussed in Chapter 4 there are many myths around money, particularly about its origin in precious metal. Seeing money as originally taking the form of a gold or silver coin with intrinsic value produces a very different theory from seeing all money as a tangible or intangible representation of a promise of value. While the former approach tends to a 'hard' view of money, the second sees money as only a token of social, public or commercial value. The textbook view of money defines it mainly by its functions in a market economy: means of exchange, means of account, store of value, means of payment. More socially oriented approaches see the emphasis on money's role in exchange (assumed to be trade in commodities) as too limiting. Instead, they argue that money is useful as a means of account in many different contexts, including social and public arenas (Zelizer 1994). The different meanings attached to money will affect how it is seen as operating in its role of representing value. While commercial views of money will always stress value in money terms as profit, (money invested to make more money), social and public forms of money can address outcomes in terms of social and public benefit. Money means very different things, such as a gift, a fine or a commercial payment. This requires different ways of assessing value.

While commercial value is judged in the marketplace, social value will be judged in terms of personal relationships, while public value can be judged at the ballot box or in public debate, as will be discussed in the next chapter.

Many people concerned with building more ecologically sustainable and socially just sufficiency provisioning economies argue that this could be best achieved through local provisioning (Hines 2000), that 'small is beautiful' (Schumacher 1973). Advocates of alternative monetary systems want to decentralise currencies to the lowest level possible (Lietaer 2001: 266) with many advocating local money or socially created exchange mechanisms (Seyfang 2011, Cato 2012). The aim is for local production and exchange to 'short-circuit' the wider money system (Douthwaite 1996). Social money here is taken to mean money that has no status as legal tender. If in note form, it is known as scrip. What lessons does social money have for the discussion of public money in this book?

Social Money: Possibilities and Limitations

Money is contrived by a group to measure, collect and redistribute resources.

(Desan 2014: 6)

Social money comes in various forms. One approach is to create a local socially generated currency that is parallel, or complementary, to the official currency. This encourages local exchange and takes the necessity to make a profit out of the system. The money is not lent into circulation but is generally bought (with national currency) or earned. UK examples are the Bristol pound and the Totnes pound. Local exchange can also be achieved without a tangible or intangible currency. The best-known example of a scheme that relies on membership and accounting, rather than a tangible currency, is a LETS (Local Exchange Trading System). LETS are membership organisations where people carry out tasks or trade with each other coordinated by a central record (Raddon 2003, North 2007). However, as North points out, there are limitations to local trading systems.

If they require records to be kept of each interaction, they cannot operate with large numbers.

One way to have a fixed measure of value is to make time the currency. A well-known example is the Time dollar. Time dollars are earned by giving a timed service to another person. This has been successful in Japan, where Hureai Kippu (caring relationship tickets) are used for care of the elderly (Douthwaite 1999: 5). Care-givers can accumulate healthcare credits for their own use, or they can transfer their credit to others, for example to obtain care for relatives living in another part of the country. An early example of a time-based currency was established in the town of Ithaca in New York state. Currency notes, 'Ithaca Hours', were issued denominated by time, from a quarter of an hour to two hours, but also valued at the national average hourly wage. Ithaca Hours enter the economy by being issued as loans or grants to charities, or payments to those who advertise in the movement's directory of local businesses (Raddon 2003: 13).

An example of social money that the economist Paul Krugman is fond of using is the babysitting circle, although he sees it as the basic model of a commodity exchange system, rather than as an exchange of reciprocal use value (2008: 17). Babysitting circles operate on time-based exchange usually mediated by tokens. It would be possible to organise the circle on the basis of simple reciprocity without the tokens. Each parent would keep track of what they were 'owed' from the other parents. However, misunderstandings could easily arise and it would be difficult to transfer value (I can't babysit for you tonight but Steve owes me from last week, so you could try him and say I am transferring my claim on him to you, but then you will owe me...). The most straightforward way to operate the circle is for someone to cut up a sheet of card into small tokens valued at one hour or half an hour. That is, a simple social money system. The tokens are issued free of debt and form the basis for 'trading', although people might 'tax' themselves some tokens to provide support for a single parent. None of this would work if the tokens were initially lent to each parent. In the absence of any new tokens coming into the circle (new members) the tokens would dry up as they were returned to the 'banker'. It is the debt-free nature of the original tokens that makes it a sustainable system. What matters is that there are sufficient tokens to represent the likely level of activity. In the original study Krugman discusses, requests for babysitting dried up because there were not enough tokens and people hoarded them.

There are two main limits to social money: one economic, one political. Economically, local money faces the problem of scale. While the babysitting circle is a self-contained provisioning system, people need a wide range of resources for general provisioning. Alternative exchange systems tend to be limited to services, labour and small-scale production. As North points out, local systems can only work within those resources and activities they can harness (2007: 178). To be successful, a local or regional money system needs to rest on a viable local resource system, but this depends on the pattern of local ownership and control of resources. The most successful social money systems are specific rather than general, such as the Swiss WIR system that has operated between businesses since 1934.

The problem for social money is the need for public authority behind money. Many local money schemes including the WIR are backed by public currency. One important aspect of the authority of public currency is its acceptance in payment of taxes. The classic example of the importance of integration of social money into the local public economy is the Worgl scrip of 1932. Worgl is a small town in Austria that had one third unemployment in 1932. The mayor, Michael Unterguggenberger, created around 10,000 schillings in scrip notes backed by national currency. Following the principles of Silvio Gesell (1862–1930), the scrip was subject to demurrage, that is, to a decline in value over time. To maintain their value the scrip notes had to be stamped for a small fee each month. This was an encouragement to spend the notes quickly thereby increasing economic activity. The money was issued as wages to city employees and to pay for public works. In turn the scrip money was accepted by the city in payment of local taxes. The scrip money was a great success, circulating much more quickly than the national currency, and unemployment fell by 25 per cent. Several hundred similar schemes emerged, particularly in the US (Douthwaite and Wagman 1999: 97). Most were closed down by national governments as they feared that the monetary system was being 'democratised out of its hands' (1999: 100).

A local perspective on money cannot only be concerned with self-contained initiatives at the local level; it needs to confront the role of money at the national and international level. Although green economists would ideally want to align money systems with ecological systems such as bioregions (Cato 2012), this is not how money systems are traditionally located. While local money initiatives can attempt to embed a money system within a locality, in practice, democratising existing money systems will need to achieve change at the national level, or in the case of the Eurozone at the cross-national level. The need to link with the wider money system has led to proposals for plural currencies, with local money being seen as one among many, ranging from the local to the global. Richard Douthwaite sees room for four currencies, local, national and international, with a special currency for savings (1999: 53).

Money and Value

At present, capitalism appears to have won what John McMurtry calls the 'value war' between the global market economy and the 'life economy'. As a result: 'The livelihoods of millions are discarded as "uncompetitive". Life security for whole societies is abolished as "unaffordable". Financial war is waged against the welfare state' (McMurtry 2002: 4). In the world of TINA only one form of value is recognised: profitable exchange in the marketplace. This ignores the existence of many other forms of market based on different values: 'the community exchange market, the traditional public market, the non-monetised barter market, the socialist market, the local exchange-currency market and so on' (2002: 91).

The definition of money adopted in this book sees it as a representation of value that can be used in social, public and commercial contexts. While public currency has a nominal value, it embodies very different kinds of substantive value depending upon the context. In social contexts, capitalist market values may be irrelevant. A thoughtful but inexpensive gift may be more highly valued than an expensive but inappropriate one. The same is true of local provisioning contexts where exchange of value may be very fluid with no notion of maximising profit. Widespread participation is much more important than achieving market equivalence. Each person will contribute what they can. In the UK many consumer co-operative societies historically charged relatively high prices, but returned up to 25 per cent of the value as a member dividend. Co-operative members used this as a form of saving.

In a non-capitalist context, creating, attaining and holding money is not an end in itself. Money or some kind of notation is a convenience rather than a measure of profitable exchange. The aim is not to maximise money value, but to maximise social or ecological value. The money or accounting system is symbolic of participation in a provisioning community. It enables exchange that is reciprocal rather than commercial: maximising social and use value not profit. What the examples of social money demonstrate is that money systems do not have to be based on commodity values (values on the market). The commercial rate for babysitting may be £10 per hour or £5 per hour, but it makes no difference to the use value of the babysitting tokens. The tokens as a form of money serve the provisioning process, rather than the provisioning process serving the aim of accumulating tokens. Similarly public expenditure should be judged by public service value not capitalist market value. Maximising of monetary value does not mean that maximum social or environmental benefit has been achieved. In fact, it may mean quite the opposite.

If social or public monetary exchange can express use values in provisioning, where does that leave Marx's distinction between use value and exchange value? This would seem to separate use value from monetary exchange. Use value is the value of the good or service in itself. Exchange value sets up a comparative measure of commodified value in which money is the universal equivalent, the pivot around which comparative values can be established. The use of money in social and public provisioning need not imply the capitalist form of exchange based on commodification. Aligning money with commodification was certainly important to Marx as it opens his study of Capital, but he sees two forms of exchange. The first is simple commodity exchange C – M – C (commodity exchanged for money which is exchanged for a different commodity). In this model, the aim is to seek another commodity or service by providing something that can be exchanged for the money to buy that good or service. This could be seen as an exchange of use values without recourse to the notion of profit.

Marx's main critique is directed at profit-seeking exchange where the aim is not to buy a good or service, but to achieve a profit in money terms. M – C – M+ where money is invested to purchase or create commodities, goods and services that can be sold on for more money than initially invested. Under financialisation the process is taken a stage further to M – M – M+ where money is invested in money commodities to create more money. It is clear that M – C – M+ and M – M – M+ exist entirely to make a profit. However C – M – C is less clear cut. Certainly money is the means of establishing and transferring value, but the aim is not necessarily mercenary. The fact that money acts as a medium of exchange does not mean it is a medium for the extraction of profit nor that simple commodity exchange (as use-value exchange) need necessarily lead to a full-blown capitalist market. Forms of exchange that use social money are not set up to enable the extraction of profit. In fact, the monetary/exchange system would soon collapse if someone in the system were to demand more services, resources or exchange medium than they were willing to contribute. Equally, hoarding the money and not participating would undermine provisioning.

Social exchange mechanisms work on the assumption of reciprocity, rough parity, a sense of fair play and good will. Money is being used to exchange goods and services because they are what others can use and benefit from. Part of the confusion in Marx's model lies in calling the goods and services commodities in the simple C – M – C form of exchange. This implies that the goods and services are valued not for their beneficial use, but for their monetary value. Using the example of social or public money a better expression would be P – M – P. Provisioning – Money – Provisioning. Money still acts as the universal equivalent. It can bring strangers into contact and be transferred between holders. However, rather than maximising the accumulation of profit, the aim would be to maximise provisioning. Social or public money could be a highly efficient mechanism for exchanging use value. As money plays a very different role in the P – M – P model, it represents a very different approach to money from that envisaged by handbag economics. In the P – M – P model, money is not created as debt. It is created and circulated to enable maximum sufficiency provisioning. Rather than Gross Domestic Product, the measure would be Gross Domestic Provisioning.

The aim of ecologically sustainable sufficiency provisioning is to enable people, as far as possible, to set up and work in activities relevant to their well-being and flourishing. The examples of social experiments with social money and local provisioning show that alternative ways of sustaining human communities are possible. However, there are also limits to localism in terms of the availability of resources. Social money systems also appear to be most successful when they are backed by a public authority or by public money. It is therefore the argument of this book that the most appropriate form of money for sufficiency provisioning is publicly created and circulated money that prioritises use value and democratic control. How this would work is the subject of the next chapter.

3

Provisioning Through Public Money

The concept of public money can be approached in two ways. One is to address the creation and circulation of money as a public question, particularly the funding of public expenditure. The second is more specific, to explore public money as a particular form of money creation and circulation, that is, the creation of public currency free of debt.

It would be hard to imagine a contemporary society that could provision itself without money, unless it was decentralised into small face to face communities. It is also clear from the 2007–8 crisis that while the money supply in contemporary money systems has largely been privatised, it relies on periodic public rescue. Contemporary money systems are public because the public, taken to mean all the people within that money system, are affected by, and ultimately responsible for, its functioning. Money has been created in their name as publicly backed currency, that is tokens or records that express a range of entitlements or obligations. In this book public currency is defined as a readily accepted representation of a publicly authorised nominal unit of value that can be used to express actual obligations and entitlements whether they be social, public or commercial.

At its most basic, nominal money is social in that it is based on social trust. Most societies have had some form of tangible or intangible money that is socially accepted as expressing relative values. Even the value of 'hard' forms of money, such as precious metal coinage, generally relies on social trust or public authority. It is rare that forms of money have directly represented value, that is, been made of a marketable or usable commodity that reflects their exact nominal value. Most money is not a value in itself, but a promise of future acceptance of its notional value. Notes, coins, bank accounts, cards all represent a nominal value, the unit of public currency, which can be transferred as required. Money is social, because it links even strangers together in frameworks of trust (if I accept this notional value today, someone else will honour it tomorrow), with the ultimate backing of public monetary authorities.

Saying that public currencies are backed by public authority does not mean there is democratic accountability. Throughout its history publicly designated money, particularly coinage, has mainly been controlled by autocratic rulers or ruling groups. Public money as national currency has also been an important element in the emergence of nation states, regardless of the framework of governance that is adopted. However, the privatisation and ideological capture of the supply of public currency under modern capitalism obscures the social and public nature of money. The first step towards reclaiming public money for sufficiency provisioning is to raise the control of public currency as a matter for public debate.

Money as a Public Question

Money issuance has a pre-allocative and pre-distributive function.

(Huber 2014: 42)

While money can be created socially (local money) and privately (Bitcoin), the main form of money in modern economies is the public currency. While local money or private money may have a social or economic impact, they are not a public liability or a public responsibility. However, if either became large scale, there could well be political implications and demand for a public rescue when, rather than if, problems arose. Modern public currencies and public monetary authorities have emerged to deal with the need to regularise commercial money systems. The contemporary association of money with the commercial, and particularly the banking and financial sector, does not remove it from public responsibility, as the crisis showed. The supply of public currency has been privatised under handbag economics, but the public still has to sustain and support the monetary system. At present, commercial banks benefit from that support, with little public accountability. As noted earlier, Martin Wolf and Felix Martin have both argued that the present commercial banks, in their role as supplier of money, should be seen as an unregulated form of civil service, given that they rely so heavily on state support.

It is widely recognised that the majority of modern money supply is based on money created as debt. The figure of 97 per cent for the UK is often reported (Jackson and Dyson 2012: 16). This figure is derived from the money represented by bank accounts as against money represented as notes and coin. This does not necessarily mean that all the money in bank accounts is debt-based, as some will have originated in publicly generated money as described below. However, given the pressure of handbag economics, and the rapid increase in privately generated money in the last few decades, it is a fair assumption that most of the money sitting in bank accounts represents an origin in debt. What is important is that the money created by banks as debt is not private money. The new money created through loans is designated as public currency: pounds, dollars, euros. It is public currency privately created: a privately constructed but socially and publicly sustained promise of future acceptance in exchange for goods, services, assets or payment of obligations.

Public currency creation through unregulated private borrowing removes any democratic accountability. Creditworthiness and profitability are the most relevant criteria for money issue in a debt-based money system, which means that many sections of the population are excluded (Fuller and Mellor 2008). In market economies, the only way people can exercise 'voice' is through their ability to purchase goods and services, which requires access to money. Capitalist ideology has captured economic reasoning in relation to money supply. If people seek money for social and ecological expenditure, they will be told that 'this cannot be afforded' as it is not profitable. The only solution to demands for social justice is the promise of growth; that given time the debt-fuelled market will lift all boats. The pretence is that the market puts some kind of brake on money creation and allocates it most efficiently. The recent crisis shows that neither of these claims is true.

What was remarkable in the response to the crisis was the lack of mainstream proposals to control the banks. Some have been made – such as a Financial Transactions Tax to inhibit low return high frequency trading, and splitting of banking activities – but these do not address what banks actually do. As many theorists of money have explained, banks do not lend depositor's money, they create money deposits by making loans (Ryan-Collins et al. 2011: 117). The problem is that in doing so they create the nation's money supply, and therefore cannot be allowed to fail. The simplest way to remove bank-created debt and its growth dynamic is to remove from the banking system the right to create new public currency, or to severely limit it. Banks would be restricted to doing what most people think they do: lend savers' existing money to borrowers. Instead of money created through bank-issued debt, new public money could be issued by public monetary authorities, free of debt, directly into the economy to meet public needs. According to handbag economics, public expenditure has to wait for the commercial circulation of money before it can be taxed. That is, public expenditure relies on monetary growth in the commercial sector. Most people cannot produce directly the goods and services they need, they first have to work in private profit-driven or public profit-dependent activities to obtain access to money.

Money as a Public Resource

Given the public nature of money as evidenced by the banking and financial crisis and the resulting public liability, the logic would be that all money should be seen as a public resource (Mellor 2010a: 167). A crucial social and political question would then be: who has the benefit of that resource? To see money as a public resource rather than a privately generated medium would demand political action around the public currency. It may be that given a voice over money supply the public would vote to give the administration of money back to the private sector, but it would be much more likely that public and social expenditure would be prioritised. The private sector would then have to re-orient its activities to serving publicly determined priorities. This could form the basis of a provisioning system where growth would only occur in response to expressed need. Money circulation could be focused on the sufficiency provisioning of socially necessary goods and services, ensuring enough for all, rather than a surfeit for some.

The financial crisis has provided the opportunity to re-evaluate current money and financial systems from a green and social justice perspective. Public currency could be the means of exchanging use value, necessary goods and services, while avoiding unnecessary work and consumption. The present profit-driven system is unable to reduce or eliminate resource depletion and environmental damage, or take account of the intrinsic value of the natural world. A money system based on debt cannot enable an ecologically sustainable economy, or provision societies on sufficiency principles, because it is subject to constant expansion driven by commercial forces. Money is not a neutral economic instrument, it is a social and political force. Public creation and circulation of money, free of debt, under democratic control, could enable the provisioning of large-scale societies on the basis of social justice and ecological sustainability (Robertson 2012).

Often public money is taken to mean public expenditure, but this does not explain the source of the money that is being spent. Under handbag economics all the money committed to public expenditure is assumed to have come directly, or indirectly, from corporate or individual taxpayers. This money must have originated as debt-based money through the banking system, as according to handbag economics, there can be no public source of new money. However, this view, that all money should be seen as private (belonging to individuals and companies), is undermined by the scale of the bailout and the need for new money to be created by public monetary authorities.

Despite the household analogy peddled by handbag economics, conventional money and banking theory does recognise the ability of central banks to create public currency. In fact, it sees this as superior to bank-created money. Banks are seen as creating a lower quality of money, 'credit money', while central-bank-created new money is described as 'high powered money' or 'base money'. This confusion at the heart of handbag economics points to its weakness as an economic framework that will be explored in later chapters. Key to the critique is the pivotal role of the central bank between the rest of the public sector and the commercial banks. Handbag economics rejects the public creation of public currency ('printing money') because it denies the possibility of using money to generate social and public value. It maintains that social and public expenditure cannot create value, because it does not create profit, that is, money invested in commodity exchange to create more money (M – C – M+). Value is seen as only emerging in a commercial circuit (investment/borrowing – production/services – profit/repayment/interest). Public goods and services are a by-product of the search for profit. This ignores the fact that there is also a public circuit of money that enables public value to be created in terms of goods and services delivered for public benefit. There are then two circuits: the commercial and the public.

The Commercial Circuit of Money

Neoliberal economics recognises only one circuit of money. Money is invested in, or lent to, the private sector to enable wealth creation. Banks act as intermediaries between savers or investors and the wealth creators. The possibility of banks creating new money is not generally acknowledged. When goods and services are sold and/or profits are made, lenders and investors are repaid. Workers get wages which they can spend on goods and services or deposit/save to support future production. Under handbag economics, the public sector can access this money either by borrowing from the banking and financial sector (the money markets) or taxing the public and private sectors.

In the ideal capitalist scenario, money creation through bank lending does not play a role. A stock of money is assumed to be already in existence. It is borrowed, invested successfully and returned to the bank or other bond-holder with interest. Because debt is tax deductible for companies it makes sense to be 'maxed out' (Scurlock 2007). For individuals and households, who cannot offset their debt payments against tax, there is understandable frustration as they try to repay debts and pay taxes. From the borrowers' perspective there appears to be no choice about repaying debt, while tax is seen as a political imposition. Taxation then becomes a political football, while the need to repay bank debt remains unchallenged.

The ideological hegemony of neoliberal handbag economics, and dominance of the private money circuit, has led to an attack on postwar welfare states and public sector investment. Public expenditure is undermined by the claim that the taxpayer is being robbed by wasteful governments. The rich demand lower taxes to support their 'entrepreneurship' or threaten to take their money elsewhere. Tax avoidance is rife and very few governments dare raise taxes. As Andrew Sayer (2014) argues, the public can no longer afford the rich. Financialised capitalism is profiting without producing, and one of its major sources of profit is household debt (Lapavitsas 2013). Rather than contributing to the provision of goods and services through productive investment, the rich extract resources and hoard their money. This is what Keynes feared and led to his demand that governments seek to maintain full employment when capitalist investment failed. As the rich do not carry out the basic money circulation function of employing labour to produce, there is little money outside of the financial sector. This has resulted in huge inequalities between millionaire earnings and bonus-enhanced salaries in the financial gambling arena, and zero hours contracts with unemployment or underemployment elsewhere. As Piketty (2014) has argued, the concentration of wealth and growing inequality is stifling the growth of capitalism itself.

The neoliberal aim of reducing taxation of the commercial money circuit has led to pressure on public services. The public then experiences frustration at limited or poor service. A democratic deficit emerges as people see elected bodies as 'doing nothing for us' and being 'as bad as each other'. Similarly, the employed are turned against the unemployed and other welfare recipients. Everything is presented as a zero-sum game: your benefit is my tax. Again, money is assumed to be a limited resource that can only legitimately be used by the 'wealth creators' even when they are bonus-driven, speculative, derivative traders. David Harvey (2014) sees the limited profitable investment opportunities for the vast accumulation of speculative money capital as a major contradiction for capitalism. It has led to endless financial 'innovations' to soak up the excess money. As has been shown, the commercial circuit of money must inevitably end in crisis as people, businesses and governments become over-indebted. Public creation of money is then necessary if the privatised money supply system is to be rescued. However, despite the capacity of monetary authorities to create the public currency free of debt, public expenditure above the level of taxation is designated as a deficit, requiring more public debt, resulting in the imposition of austerity on the public budget.

The Public Circuit of Money

Despite the protestations of neoliberal economists, public money is continually being created and spent in a public sector circuit, reflecting the long history of sovereign creation of money. Much early coinage was created free of debt and spent, mainly on war or aggrandisement. The money was then left to circulate or demanded back as tax. When modern bank lending emerged, rulers combined public money creation and taxation with borrowing from the commercial money sector and the sources of public funding became intertwined.

The public circuit is obscured because public expenditure is an ebb and flow of money. States do not wait to collect taxes before engaging in expenditure. It is only when outgoings and tax income are brought together in the accounts that the balance between them can be seen. The sequence of taxation and expenditure is therefore circular: taxes are spent and expenditure is taxed. Rather than seeing the circuit starting with tax to fund expenditure, expenditure can be seen as providing money to pay taxes. The 'chicken and egg' nature of the public circuit creates further confusion over the role of the central bank (or equivalent public authority such as the Treasury). The central bank/Treasury can be seen as lending/borrowing money for public expenditure pending the receipt of taxes, or it can be seen as creating money for public expenditure that will be redeemed through taxation. If the public monetary authority behaves like a commercial bank, it will see this money as a loan to the state. Future taxation is then a fiscal matter of retrieving the money to repay the loan (with interest). If the monetary authority sees itself as a public agency, the public currency could be created debt free, and spent pending possible future taxation.

Depending on how the public money circuit is interpreted, the incoming tax can be seen as being drawn from activities in the private sector (based on commercial wealth creation) or it can be seen as the state's own expenditure being returned. Given that in modern economies there is both public and commercial creation of public currency, both are true. Both circuits can be seen as creating value by providing goods and services. While the commercial sector extracts its value as price on the market, the value of the public sector is judged by the quality of its provisioning.

If the creation of public currency is not through the commercial sector, money doesn't need to be made out of money. Unlike bank-created money, publicly created public currency doesn't have to be commodified. It can be spent or allocated as a public resource without the need to be returned (with profit). However, it is not wise to create unlimited amounts of money (memo to the banking sector before the crash). The public money circuit is therefore completed not by repayment of debt, but by payment of taxes or fees. Tax in this case is not a fiscal instrument as in the commercial money circuit (raising taxes from individuals, households and companies for the public sector to spend) but a monetary instrument, to retrieve money from circulation that could otherwise be inflationary. This creates a very different position for the taxpayer. Instead of 'hardworking families' paying out their 'hard-earned money' in taxes, they can be seen as returning money that has done its work in creating public benefit (paying doctors, building bridges, environmental work, care for the elderly).

The main difference between the commercial and public circuits of money is that publicly created money *may* be issued as debt, but bank-created money can *only* be issued as debt.

Rethinking Deficit

Recognising the public circuit of money puts deficit spending in a new light. Running a deficit does not need to put the public sector into the red as handbag economics dictates. A deficit means that the public sector is spending more money than it is taking back in tax. How this is perceived depends on whether the source of money is seen as emerging from the public or the commercial circuit of money. The role of the central bank is critical here. If the extra money is seen as being 'borrowed' from the central bank it will be sold on to the financial sector and added to the national debt. Seeing the central bank as exercising the sovereign prerogative to create money would allow the additional money to circulate debt free. If the 'deficit' is not taxed, it can filter into the private sector and be a net gain to the economy as a whole. Quite the opposite occurs when handbag economics asks the public sector to balance the books, or, worse, go into surplus. If the public sector takes more in tax and payments than it spends, it is extracting money from the economy.

Far from being a problem, there *needs* to be a public deficit. Creation by public authorities of money that is not reclaimed is necessary, otherwise the privatised money supply will go into crisis as a purely debt-based money supply is not sustainable. Rather than demanding an end to budget deficits, they should be seen as a key element of macroeconomic policy in creating financial stability (Arestis and Sawyer 2010). As Wray argues, 'if government emits more in its payments than it redeems in taxes, currency is accumulated by the non-government sector as financial wealth' (2011: 7); 'affordability is never the issue, rather the real debate should be over the proper role of government, how it should use the monetary system to achieve public purpose' (2011: 17). Given the public ability to create or withdraw money, there should be no problem with the stock of money in the economy. Flow is the problem, too much or too little. What is needed is counter-cyclical state action to support employment, if necessary as employer of last resort: 'a government that issues its own currency has the fiscal and monetary policy space to spend enough to get the economy to full employment' (Wray 2012: 194).

Suggesting that the state should reclaim its money-creation power will almost inevitably be met by the assertion that the issue of debt-free public currency risks inflation. This ignores the monetary role of taxation; as Galbraith has pointed out, fiscal policy can be used to manage excess demand as well as managing falling demand (1975: 306–7). If more money is issued than can be absorbed by the level of goods and services in the economy, taxation can be used to retrieve that money. Critics of states 'printing money' tend to ignore the inflationary pressures of the floods of bank-issued debt that have led to a series of asset-price booms. Good and bad management of money can occur in both state-based and bank-based money creation.

The irony of handbag economics and its emphasis on the importance of the 'money markets' in financing the public sector is that public debt, far from being a problem, is an essential asset for the financial sector. Against the claims of handbag economics that high levels of state debt will create high interest rates, one of the most sought after forms of investment in unstable situations is state debt, despite often low interest rates. This is particularly the case where countries have their own currency, but even bailout countries such as Portugal were able to return to the commercial markets at a reasonable rate of interest relatively quickly.

Reclaiming the public ability to create money free of debt would threaten the safe state investments that many financial institutions such as pension funds require. However, pension funds would not be so necessary if people could be sustained by a citizens income funded by debt-free money (see below). This would also reduce the wider growth demands of the pension funds and financial industries generally. It would solve the top-heavy problem of ageing populations needing to extract profitable investments from a shrinking working-age population.

The 'money markets' also constantly threaten public sustainability as they surcharge state debt or threaten currencies. As will be discussed in Chapter 7, there is the difficult question of states investing in each other's debt and other assets. It would be much less complicated if the majority of public expenditures were administered within an internal public money circuit. Most importantly, selling public deficits as debt is socially unjust as repayment of that debt falls on the public while the investments are mainly a source of benefit to the already wealthy who can directly or indirectly 'buy' the debt. Under the public circuit, the money would be removed through taxation. The choice between additional taxation or increasing national debt is highly ideological and goes to the heart of modern public finance.

Given the public responsibility that the existence of a public currency entails, the question also needs to be raised as to what responsibility to the public the holders of money have. People in a monetary system sit on both sides of that relationship, as holders of entitlements to goods, services or assets, but also of obligations for private and public payments. The privatisation of the creation of money obscures one side of that relationship. Holding money is seen as representing a personal entitlement, while the public obligations that are entailed are ignored, even rejected by handbag economics. The public currency (the pound in your pocket) is seen as representing only the private creation of wealth, a personal asset, there is no sense of it representing a public obligation or the need for a collective commitment to creating public wealth.

Public Money as Public Wealth

Capitalism has captured the definition of economic wealth as profit and accumulation measured in monetary terms. Capitalist expansion is based upon the new creation of 'credit money' (debt) or the transfer of money already in circulation ('idle money' or loanable funds). Commercial wealth is created through the use of that money to enable labour, resources and knowledge to be employed to produce goods or services that are then purchased with existing money or further borrowings. The overall aim is to increase total money value with the benefit accruing to owners, investors and senior managers/executives before 'trickling down' to the rest of the population. Under financialisation, the evidence is that money has become concentrated rather than distributed (Dorling 2014, Weeks 2014).

As discussed in the previous chapter, a commodified view of wealth creation is not a suitable basis for sufficiency provisioning. Rather than maximising commodity value, the aim of the public money circuit would be to create value in terms of the goods and services delivered. That is, common wealth not private wealth. Publicly created money could prioritise use value and aim for one-step provisioning where people would work as far as possible on participation in the provision of goods and services the population would need and use. Rather than defining wealth in terms of market value, provisioning priorities need to be set in democratic debate. Wealth would not be measured by the accumulation of money, but by the security of social provisioning: the capacity of the public non-commercial economy to deliver goods and services.

The creation of public money would not be limited by the pressures of the 'money market' but would be determined by total social need. This would not preclude the existence of a commercial market, but it would not be the basis of the public money supply. The level of provision of public services would be driven by the quantity and quality of service needed. Local users of that service would judge the value for money spent. Wasteful duplication of providers would be avoided, and there would be a presumption of collective public or social provision for basic needs. The question then becomes whether the circulation of money will be completed by immediate payment for the services, by later taxation, or be funded through non-inflationary monetary expansion, that is, surplus public spending (defined as a deficit by handbag economics).

Failure to recognise the value of public wealth has led to the mass privatisation of public services, particularly in the UK. Seeing local services such as post offices as businesses led to privatisation and mass closures because they were not 'profitable' in immediate financial terms (Large 2010: 34). Amartya Sen points to the way that public services such as universal healthcare and education can support overall wealth, including conventional economic growth (*Guardian*, 6 January 2015). The particular case he cites is Kerala in India, which was once one of the poorest states. It took the political decision to provide universal services and is now one of the more prosperous states (Dreze and Sen 2014). He cites Rwanda as another poor country that has successfully expanded basic healthcare. Sen points out that, even in conventional terms, public services can be afforded in poor countries because health and education are highly labour intensive. Cuba has achieved a world-renowned capacity in medicine as it was one of the few areas it could expand without requiring high levels of external resources, particularly following the collapse of its main supporter, the Soviet Union.

Welfare provision, being labour intensive, delivers money into the local economy. Often poor communities experience an acute shortage of money, as very little of the money earned stays local. Most supplies come from external sources, as do most of the costs (rent, utilities, etc). Expanding the public circuit of money through locally provided provisioning would encourage the local social and commercial circulation of money. Both locally and nationally, public service provision could become the major source of money wealth, reversing the position today where commercial activities are perceived to be the only source of wealth for the public sector. Wealth would be judged by the quality of the environment and the security of provisioning. The overall aim would be that the need to accumulate money wealth or asset wealth would be removed. Once people were assured that the source of public money could never dry up, they would not feel the need to maximise their income or hoard money. Sufficiency provisioning would mean that products that required the use of natural resources would become more expensive, but labour intensive activities such as culture and entertainment could expand. This could create an enhanced conviviality of public life.

Democratising Money

As argued above, taking debt out of the public money supply would enable social and public provisioning to be prioritised, and remove the destructive growth dynamic inherent in handbag economics. Most importantly, it could provide the basis for democratically determined, socially just, sufficiency provisioning. First, there is a need to recognise the capacity of public monetary authorities to create money. The bailout showed that central banks can create new money at will, but neoliberal ideology demands that the money only be directed towards the banking sector. There is no reason why publicly created money should not be allocated to a wide range of provisioning agents, or to nature itself, as an income to enable ecological sustainability. Examples of social money show that money can be distributed in various ways, for a variety of purposes, adopting alternative concepts of value. It is the hegemony of capitalist economic thinking that denies a social and public right to a livelihood outside of wage labour. Seeing money as only related to the process of commodification denies the possibility of recognising the alternative of social and public money in the exchange of use value.

Green thinkers have long argued that the right to create the public currency must be removed from the banking sector (Robertson 2012, Robertson and Bunzl 2003, Huber and Robertson 2000, Douthwaite 1999). Banks would retain a utility function, but no longer be able to create new money through bank loans. They would take not-for-loan deposits, and provide services linked to money circulation (payments, transfers, etc). Banks could also provide personal, social, public and commercial loans targeted at agreed priorities, using money created by the central bank. Other investments and speculative finance would be entirely private, with no access to loans from banks. Any money invested would be at risk. Stripped of its 'leverage', the present financial sector would necessarily shrink through lack of new money. This could be aided by a wealth tax to remove the profits created by previous speculative activity. The private sector might then retrench in favour of commercial activities linked more to the provision of goods and services. As the commercial money circuit shrank, the public money circuit would need to be expanded sufficiently to ensure that remaining socially responsible commercial provisioning was not undermined by lack of money.

Banks based on a public service ethos and public, social or co-operative structures would be more appropriate for a sufficiency investment system, where the priority is the delivery of a good or service rather than the return on capital invested (Mellor 2012b, Brown 2013). There is evidence that co-operative banks were, with some notable exceptions, better able to withstand the financial crisis. Bajo and Roelants argue on international evidence that 'through their systematic accumulation of common reserves, combined with participatory dynamics, co-operatives provide a model for firms not to fall into the "debt trap"' (2011: 221). They found co-operatives built up counter-cyclical buffers, had more capital, made better provision against risk and had low insolvency ratios because they lent against a real capacity to pay. They lend more to local SMEs and local productive entities such as farms. Co-operatives tended to accumulate productive capital, not speculative capital, and did not encourage clients to make speculative investments (Bajo and Roelants 2011: 215–6).

In the recent crisis, however, co-operative and publicly owned banks were not without problems where they embraced the same business models as the commercial banks. Structures were not enough. The British Co-operative Bank rode the crisis well until it took over a failing building society that had made unwise loans. This led to massive losses and the bank fell into the hands of a hedge fund. A more successful example is the North Dakota state bank. Set up in 1919, North Dakota is the only state-owned bank in the US. It was founded when a radical movement, the Nonpartisan League, took over the legislature and founded the bank to enable the mainly agricultural population to escape from loan sharks. It acts somewhat like a state central bank in its relationship with local commercial banks, but it does take retail deposits. As it mainly administers state accounts, and avoided financial innovation and speculation, the bank survived the crisis well.

It is therefore not sufficient just to take the current banking system into social or public ownership, since publicly or socially owned banks can be as seduced by the speculative financial business model as the commercial banks. Public ownership under current concepts of economic development is unlikely to provide the basis for provisioning sufficiency. Many of the publicly owned banks around the world are based on the aim of achieving economic development in conventional terms, as in China. They may be funded by public money, but they follow the debt-based money model. Loans may be better directed and more socially responsive, but the viability of the banks is still related to the market. They are part of the commercial monetary circuit, not the public monetary circuit. Better examples of socially based finance are the many credit unions, co-operative and community finance revolving loan funds. However they are still based on debt, as is the microcredit movement (Affleck and Mellor 2006). What matters is not just the ownership structure but the values driving the banking system.

One way to democratise money would be to put it directly into people's hands.

Citizen Income

Provisioning could be democratised through a universal citizen income or basic income. The case for a citizen income can be traced back to Thomas Paine who argued that the earth was a common heritage for everyone and that each should have their share. This represents a major change that would see access to money as a citizen right, rather than being linked to an obligation to earn. Seeing waged labour as the means of access to sustenance cannot be the basis of sufficiency provisioning as it drives unnecessary work. Keynes's aim of full employment would be better expressed as full provisioning. As Stiglitz points out, in the US only a very small proportion of the labour force is needed to produce all necessary food and exports (2010: 288). If this work were shared out, there would be ample time for the other areas of provisioning and leisure. By spreading economic power more equally, a citizen income could create demand that puts needs before discretionary or luxury expenditure. In money-based provisioning systems, money access is an issue of social justice.

Hanlon et al. present evidence that dispensing money is more successful in eliminating poverty than schemes such as microcredit, which continue to place the burden of repayment on recipients. Drawing on evidence from countries such as Brazil, Mexico, Indonesia and South Africa, they argue that citizen grants are the most progressive approach. However, to be effective they should be seen as fair in their allocation, be regular and assured, substantial enough to make a difference, well administered and have popular support. They conclude: 'to reduce poverty and promote development, just give money to the poor' (2010: 178–9).

One developed-world example of a citizen dividend is Alaska. A Permanent Fund was set up in 1976 that pays an annual dividend to eligible residents. The highest amount was over $2,000 in 2008. However, the dividend is problematic from an ecological perspective as it is based on a fund built up through the sale of natural resources, mainly petroleum. Other examples have involved distributing state surpluses or making payments to counter the effects of the crisis. Hong Kong made a one-off payment of HK$6,000 to all adult residents in 2012. In 2009 Australia made a range of one-off allowances and payments including A$900 to single-income families. The Bush administration in the US responded to the crisis through a one-off tax refund.

A citizen income can be seen as the most direct form of economic democracy as it puts financial decisions into people's hands, in the hope that they will adopt less consumer-based and income-seeking lifestyles. In particular, it provides an income for those who are not in paid employment. However, it has its limitations. The amount may not be sufficient to make a material difference and it does not meet the needs for collective expenditure such as the provision of services and infrastructure. Current suggestions of 'rolling up' existing benefits into a universal payment would penalise the poorest if it meant a reduced income. A citizen income could only be 'afforded' if money creation and circulation was through the public money circuit, and it should certainly be an element in a sufficiency provisioning system.

Participatory and Deliberative Democracy

A public money system would not be acceptable unless it was fundamentally democratic. It cannot be assumed that public authorities would necessarily use money wisely, unless they were subject to democratically based mandates and effective public scrutiny. Exclusive control of public money must not be in the hands of the government in power, or the state apparatus. Neither public nor private finance are free of embezzlement and corruption. Creation of both public and commercial money needs to be transparent and accountable. Economic democracy must be much wider than the government in power. One important point of principle is to separate debates about money creation and circulation from the expenditure of a specific government. The organisation of the economy must be participatory and deliberative at the widest level if a socially just and ecologically sustainable provisioning system is to be established.

Involvement of the public in decisions about the allocation of money would be a sea-change in what is meant by democracy. Hitherto democracy has addressed who should make decisions about the distribution of resources after they have been produced and taxed. There are a series of levels at which choices should be based on democratically determined principles. The first and most important level is an initial public debate about how money creation should be controlled. What should be the balance between the public and the commercial circuits of money? As has been seen, bank creation of debt-based public currency is not a private matter when it has implications for public liability. The public needs to be aware that there is a choice to be made, part of which concerns the overall amount of money to be created (rather than the privatised free-for-all at the moment) and which bodies should be enabled to create it. Those standing to be elected to public office at all levels should be required to make a clear statement about the allocation of the right to create money between public agencies on a debt-free basis and the banking sector creating money as debt.

Democratic involvement in the decisions about the creation and allocation of money must be very different from the indirect principles of representative democracy. The public must be brought in at the early deliberative stages (Dryzek 2010). As Panayotakis argues, 'all citizens should democratically determine their society's economic goals and priorities' (2011: 149). There is a well-established example of democratic involvement in public expenditure decisions in the participatory budgeting system in Porto Alegre, Brazil (Nylen 2003). This is based on a pyramid structure from street level upwards as people vote on spending priorities. A similar nested structure of decision-making is put forward by Nelson and Timmerman (2011). Decisions taken at the lowest level (street, household) are aggregated at the next level (locality, group of streets) and the next (city quarter, administrative district) and so on until the final aggregation (city, region or state). Their system, however, does not envisage using money.

In order to avoid centralisation and to maximise participation, budgets would as far as possible be built up convergently from the grassroots through regions to the relevant centre. While most green proposals for new ways of issuing money would favour local money creation and circulation under social control, in practice a good deal of money creation would need to remain at a broader public level. Major expenditure decisions that need to be made at the centre would then have to cascade to the grassroots. For example, the level of citizen income would need to be discussed both locally and nationally, as would levels of taxation or per capita expenditure. Specialist areas of spending would also require their own democratic structures, such as health (a combined panel of users and providers) or agriculture (consumers, retailers, producers, environmentalists). There would therefore be a two-way flow of decision-making: convergent from the local to the centre(s) and cascading from the centre(s) to the local.

A circuit view sees money as being continually removed from circulation through taxation or debt-repayment and then being re-created as expenditure or new loans. All public expenditure should therefore be regarded as new public money at the point at which it starts the public money circuit. The circuit always ends with the money creator, whether bank or state, and only they can restart the cycle. Using debt-free public money as the basis of public provisioning requires both long-term and short-term fine-tune budgeting. Major long-term decisions would need to be made about allocation to sectors, with smaller-scale adjustments on an ongoing basis. These decisions would need to be deliberative and broad-based with elected politicians as only one of the participants in the process. Democratising the creation of money would require participation at many levels with at least one independent element.

Participatory Primary Budgeting

Based on convergent and cascading deliberation about expenditure and allocation proposals, a primary public money budget would need to be established. This would aggregate the proposals in order to decide how much money would be required to meet provisioning and other publicly determined needs. What is included would be a matter for public debate, but it would reflect proposed expenditure or allocation of public money at local, regional, national and international levels. Current patterns of expenditure would be a starting point for discussion. Areas covered could include: public infrastructure and services; allocation to banks or specialist agencies for grants or lending; to communities to spend/lend/allocate; a basic income to citizens, or an income to nature. It would open up the possibility of hybrids in delivery, supervised banks making debt-free allocations or public agencies making loans to individuals or public or social enterprises.

There might be a dramatic expansion of some areas of money supply if the decision was made to fund what are now unpaid livelihoods through, for example, a citizen's income or payment of domestic and community labour. Other areas might shrink to reflect a move towards sufficiency provisioning. As this would be a complex process in the first instance, the primary money supply calculation would be for at least a five-year period, or even longer, with provision for smaller-scale adjustments when required.

Monetary Assessment

The primary budget would then be subject to an independent assessment of the monetary impact of the proposed public money supply. Shifting control of the money supply to the public money circuit would require a different monetary management. The commercial circuit based on debt has an automatic dynamic: debts must be repaid. Current monetary control has been directed at encouraging or limiting the amount of debt issued through manipulation of interest rates or direct regulation. Indirect control through interest rates has not been very successful in curbing lending. The most stable periods have been when governments have prescribed or proscribed certain kinds of lending or certain kinds of lenders and borrowers.

The public money circuit needs a different dynamic as there is no automatic mechanism for the completion of the circuit. Money created free of debt does not have the impetus of repayment. The main ways to complete the circuit would be to charge for services, to tax, or to provide the public with investment opportunities. While the balance between these would be a matter for public debate, an independent monetary authority would assess the overall amount of money that should be retrieved so as to leave enough to enable all commercial and public payments to be made while avoiding inflationary pressures. It would have no say on how the money would be reclaimed from circulation. Questions such as the level of taxes, redistribution of income and wealth, taxes on resource use or land taxes, what kinds of expenditure should be charged, or whether the public should be invited to return their money as investment or savings such as pensions would be democratically determined.

Participatory Secondary Budgeting

Actual expenditure, monitoring and allocation of money in specific communities, agencies and governments would be determined through a variety of forms of decision-making, emphasising transparency and accountability. All public and private organisations that receive a direct or indirect allocation of public money would need to have clear mechanisms for democratic accountability in place.

Such a large-scale transparent system of primary and secondary budgeting would minimise the possibility for abuse. It would certainly prevent the abuse the financial sector has exhibited: manipulation of markets and rates, insider dealing, outright fraud and excessive borrowing, among others. This is not to ignore corruption in the public sector, due to lack of transparency and abuse of power. The spread of decision-making proposed would militate against domination by any particular group or body. Setting long-term budgets would mean that governments could not substantially amend proposed money-creation levels during the run up to elections, particularly in view of the moderating role of the independent monetary authority (Mellor 2012a).

Debt-free Money for Sufficiency Provisioning

Economic democracy as proposed above would make political democracy more meaningful. Rather than periodic elections there would be the opportunity for regular debate with tangible outcomes in terms of goods and services. The approach to money and the economic framework would be very different under sufficiency provisioning. Labour as employment would not be the main access to provisioning. Money would not just represent work done, but be an entitlement to livelihood. Security of needs-led provisioning could allow people to adopt less employment-intensive and consumer-intensive lifestyles. This does not mean there would be no paid work, but under the principles of one-step provisioning people would be engaged on dem-ocratically determined priorities. As the primary source of debt-free public currency, public provisioning would become the main creator of wealth in the community, providing work, goods and services. The private sector would rely on the secondary circulation of that money into a (socially and environmentally regulated) market. Sufficiency provisioning would also require a different way to reflect and measure provisioning activities.

At present, GDP is measured in a combination of total output of goods and services, total expenditure on goods and services, and total income. It marginalises or excludes unpaid work, environmental costs, asset inflation (e.g. house price rises) and the distribution of incomes. Although the case has long been made that environmental benefits and unpaid work should be included in systems of national accounts (Waring 1989), they still play a very secondary role. Sufficiency provisioning would still need a measure of performance and many proposals have been put forward, such as happiness indexes, health, life expectancy, etc. As discussed earlier, rather than measuring Gross Domestic Product, the aim should be to capture Gross Domestic Provisioning. Rather than national aggregate measures, local accounting should reflect performance on the ground. This could include productive provisioning, environmental integrity, conviviality and sociability, quality of life, equality and levels of involvement.

Making it Happen

Getting the principle of provisioning through public money established will not be easy. Neoliberalism and handbag ideology are deeply ingrained. Politicians are distrusted. However, evidence of the inappropriateness of commercial control of the money supply and understanding of the role of public money is building. There is a growing literature to draw on (Wolf 2014, Martin 2014, Robertson 2012, Jackson and Dyson 2012, Wray 2011, Ryan-Collins et al. 2011) together with considerable debate on the web. Critique of the present system also comes from across the political spectrum, although the solutions offered are very different.

It is also important to start from current conditions, that is, with large, mainly urbanised populations. Local self-sufficiency or collective local sufficiency is unlikely to be able to provision the more than 20 million people in Mexico City. However, the principle of sufficiency provisioning is being pursued by grassroots movements such as the slow movement in Europe; via campesina (the peasant's way), a global campaign for sustainable agriculture and 'food sovereignty', enabling local communities to control their own food resources; buen vivir (living well), a movement originating in South America that promotes sustainability and indigenous people's rights to livelihood. In the UK the Transition Towns movement promotes local paths to ecological sustainability and sufficiency. Degrowth and anti-capitalist protests such as Occupy campaign against current patterns of ownership and control.

Although the wealthy have insulated themselves both physically and ideologically, the people are knocking at their gate. One way to break the stranglehold of capital is to establish the existence of the public money circuit and the need to disentangle it from the commercial circuit. Once reclaimed, the public money circuit can be used for publicly determined ends. This could involve compulsorily (re)purchasing key productive capacity or the assets of the rich using public money and then taxing them heavily on the proceeds. The claim that only capitalist firms and the rich can provide employment and generate wealth must be challenged. As the evidence Sayer (2014) and Piketty (2014) present shows, the rich are no longer performing this role (if they ever did). There is no longer any basis to the claim that the market is efficient and can bring prosperity to all. The neoliberal 'experiment' has had several unregulated decades to prove itself and failed miserably (Bowman and Froud 2014).

The public sector must no longer be blackmailed by the private sector, particularly finance. It is the private sector that is parasitical upon the public sector, not the other way around. When the debt-driven capitalist economy goes into one of its regular tailspins it runs to hide under the public mummy's apron, to use handbag economics' own analogy. Reclaiming public control of the money supply would directly challenge the ability of capitalism to survive without the power to commercially create publicly backed public currency. Finally the myths and confusions of neoliberal handbag economic ideology need to be exposed. That is the task of the next two chapters.

4

Misunderstanding Public Money: Four Myths and a Confusion

The previous chapters have explored the origin and nature of public money in three ways. The first is as a mechanism of social convention or social invention to enable the establishment and transfer of use value in terms of goods or social benefit. The second is money as a public resource based on public authority (democratic or authoritarian). This involves an extension of social trust to public trust: that the public authority will maintain and supply viable money where necessary. The third is the use of social and publicly supported money (public currency) as a means of exchange for profit. It is this commercialisation of money that has led to myths and confusions about the nature of money and obscured its social and public origins. The creation and circulation of public currencies has been hijacked by the ability of publicly licensed and supported banks to commodify the supply of money as debt. This commodification of public currency as debt has led to crisis, austerity, and an attack on public and social provisioning led by neoliberal handbag economics.

The four myths of handbag economics that have led to financial crisis and austerity are (1) that the public sector cannot create wealth and must therefore not create money; (2) that money originated in barter; (3) that the first real money was precious metal coinage; and (4) that banks are only intermediaries between savers and borrowers. The four myths are interlinked and stand or fall together. They will be explored in this chapter. The confusion about money relates to the role of the central bank and will be discussed mainly in the following chapter.

Myth 1: Public Money – No Such Thing

The first myth has already been extensively discussed. It is the myth that money must be created and controlled by the private sector because wealth can only be created by private enterprise. In reality, far from the public sector being dependent on a wealth-creating commercial sector, the bailout has clearly shown that the private sector is dependent upon the public sector to sustain the monetary mechanism through which the private sector accumulates its wealth and realises its profits. Similarly, the assertion that the public sector does not, and should not, 'print money' misunderstands the dependent nature of the private sector on the public capacity to create money, particularly in a crisis. It also creates confusion about the nature of the money produced by central banks, often described as base money or high powered money.

It is evident that the public sector *can* create money. Public monetary authorities have created huge amounts of money to rescue their banking sectors. The fact that most of this money has been lent to the banking and financial sector does not detract from its origin in the public sector. In addition, the earlier chapters have argued that the public sector can produce wealth, if wealth is defined as goods and services for the people. It does not create wealth as profit, as then it would have to extract more money from the economy than it provides. In fact, being in 'deficit' supports the ability of people to access goods and services through new money created by surplus public spending. Additional purchasing power is put in the hands of the people that can feed through into the private sector.

Myth 2: Barter Begets Money

The second myth assumes that trade is the instinctive basis of human interaction. Humans are naturally driven to 'truck and barter', as Adam Smith argued. It is assumed that in the absence of money, barter was the historic form of pre-money economy. Money is assumed to emerge from the 'inconveniences' of barter and thus give rise to fully developed markets. According to this theory, money is invented to meet the problem of the coincidence of wants in a barter economy, that is, finding someone willing to provide something you want while also wanting something you have to exchange in return. Money comes into being when one commodity enables the transfer of value from one good to another, i.e. performs the function of money as a medium of exchange.

While exchange and trade undoubtedly existed in human societies, and particularly between human societies, they were never their organising principle until the emergence of modern capitalist market economies (Graeber 2011: 28). No evidence of the extensive use of barter exists. As Polanyi pointed out, the barter-to-gold theory is a powerful origin myth: 'the alleged propensity of men to barter, truck and exchange is almost entirely apocryphal ... no economy prior to our own ... [was] ... controlled and regulated by markets' (1944/57: 44). Ingham also argues that money must logically come first: markets could not exist without a means of establishing relative value and therefore money as a unit of account is 'logically anterior and historically prior to market exchange' (2004: 25). As will be seen below, the actual history of coinage lies with rulers, not merchants.

Myth 3: Money is Good as Gold

The myth about barter leads to the assumption that money originates as a commodity. This implies that the money object has its own intrinsic value, which obscures the possibility of money having a social or public origin, or being a purely social phenomenon. The myth sees money as irrevocably tied to trade. The ideal commodity for monetary exchange is precious metal, usually taken to be gold or silver. Because the precious metal medium has its own intrinsic economic value, it allows a real transfer of value because the amount of metal transferred is assumed to be equivalent to the value of the good being bought or sold. As well as being intrinsically valuable, precious metal is durable, divisible and portable. Seeing the ideal and original form of money as intrinsically valuable sets up a challenge to all other forms of money, particularly paper, to be 'as good as gold'.

The story continues that using precious metal as money brought its own problems, particularly in ease of transport and security. The solution to the problem of security was to deposit the precious metal lumps or coins with a bank and instead trade with a paper representation of those deposits. However, this led to a temptation on the part of the banker to issue more paper than there was precious metal deposited, as they could then charge fees or interest on it. Thus a 'fractional reserve' system developed. As long as everyone doesn't want to exchange their paper for gold/silver at the same time, only the 'final payment' to settle accounts between traders need be made in the reserve metal, during the process known as 'clearing'. This became the basis of modern banking and international monetary arrangements.

This powerful and persistent view of the origin and nature of money has almost the status of a 'folk history'. Even though money is now composed of base metal, paper or electronic records, this trade and commodity-based view of money is still central to contemporary theories of money and appears in many economic textbooks. It informed monetary policy, as in the establishment of the 'gold standard'. In some quarters there is still a nostalgic desire for a modern equivalent of the 'gold standard', sometimes a desire for gold itself (Lewis 2007). Although the precious metal story of the origin of money and banking will be shown to be a misleading myth, it is not entirely wrong. Substantial amounts of money historically were made of gold and silver (or pertained to be) and people did value it as a medium of exchange. The adoption of precious metal did play a major role in the development of both modern capitalism and modern states. Gold (usually as bullion) has ended up in bank vaults for safe keeping, although mainly as the property of states.

However, precious metal coinage is only one form that money takes, and other forms of money are much older, from shells to hieroglyphs. Paper money has also been created that was not linked to metal, most notably in China. Histories of coinage have found that the face value of metal coin was rarely worth its value in metal (Innes 1913, 1914). Nor was the invention of precious metal coinage supportive of economic systems. Its scarcity often led to economic slowdowns through shortage of coin. Overabundance when a new source was found also distorted economies, as in the case of Spain after the conquest of the Americas. Even if the gold story were true it would not help in the current crisis. All the gold that has ever been mined in the world could back only a fraction of the money circulating today. In 1971, when the US finally abandoned the gold standard, it had only enough gold to cover one sixth of its dollar liabilities (Varoufakis 2011: 66).

There is also a more sinister downside to the myth of gold in the history of money. The fractional reserve explanation of the link between gold or silver as 'real money' and other seemingly less authentic monetary forms such as paper implies that those banking gold were cheating their depositors or committing usury by making commercial loans. This led to attacks on those ethnic minorities perceived as engaging in banking and lending, resulting in stereotyped images such as Shakespeare's Shylock in *The Merchant of Venice*. As will be seen this completely misrepresents the development of commercial banking. Bankers were not 'cheating' in making credit available on their own assurance. In fact, without that credit, capitalism could not have developed (Mellor 2010a: 82).

There was no historical descent from 'real' money to fiat money (based solely on social, public or commercial trust), from metallism (coins of intrinsic value) to nominalism (coins of face value). They both emerged together. Precious metal coinage was always a fluid blend of metal content and face value. However coinage was much more likely to be exchanged on the basis of count (face value) than weighing (metal content). Both the Roman and Anglo-Saxon use of coin was based on count, which the English inherited (Desan 2014: 133). A major reason was utility. Pure precious metal coinage was easily damaged and so valuable that it could not be divided into small enough units for regular use. Even the lowest value metal coinage was too valuable for everyday trade or wages.

Challenging the Myths of Barter and Gold

There are many problems with the metallist commodity theory of money. The main one is historical accuracy, particularly about the role of rulers in the origin of coinage and the emphasis on precious metal. China used base metal coins on long strings for around a thousand years, providing the origin of the word 'cash'. It did not create precious metal coins until 1890 and even then still created 'cash' until 1912 (Davies 2002: 57–8). It was not barter that gave rise to money and markets, but precious metal and other forms of coinage that enabled barter to take place and markets to emerge. As a nominal form, money is primarily social and public. People trust it because it is customary to do so, or because it is publicly authorised. The benefit of pure precious metal coinage is that there need be no trust, the commodity money is a direct expression of the value as agreed in the exchange. However, this is not using money as money, a social and public concept, but is actually barter, the direct exchange of two goods of equal value (Wray 2004: 253). The commodity is exchanged for another equivalent commodity, precious metal. But this only works if the metal can be demonstrated to be pure. The use of pure bullion or coin was mainly reserved for foreign trade or inter-state payments. Even then, a range of face value coinages and other forms of money could also be used.

In the absence of pure metal coinage, coins only have a nominal, face value. Trust and authority then necessarily enter the relationship. Although metal money was extensively used over many centuries, particularly in Europe, the link between the face value of coinage and its metal content was very haphazard (Innes, 1913, 1914, Wray 2004). In fact, rulers struggled to keep precious metal content in line with the changing face value of money. From the earliest days of metal coinage there was a struggle between the competing demands of keeping the intrinsic value of the coin and having enough coinage to circulate: 'making a metal coin that actually succeeded ... was a daunting project ... officials regularly reduced the metal content of money in order to keep it operating, a dilution that continued over many regimes and centuries' (Desan 2014: 109).

Markets did not emerge out of primitive barter through the use of intrinsic value precious metal coinage; they were socially constructed together with publicly constructed money. As Graeber points out, the development of markets relied on the active intervention of governments and the existence of public currency. Even as Adam Smith was writing about the propensity to truck and barter, the government of the day was actively developing laws and monetary policies, including increasing the money supply, to create a 'world of butchers, ironmongers and haberdashers' (Graeber 2011: 45). For Polanyi, markets are based in social frameworks, therefore 'a market economy can only function in a market society' (1944/57: 57). The real history of money is much more multifaceted than the barter-to-gold story.

Money did not emerge as a by-product of commodity exchange. It developed in social and public contexts and in many forms such as written records, shells, clay tablets, wooden tally sticks or stones (Davies 2002). While not all societies had a physical form of money, most had some form of accounting that could establish comparative value in social or public contexts such as tribute, dowry, injury payment or temple offerings. Rather than barter or markets, the earliest economies were based on 'reciprocity and redistribution' (Polanyi 1944/57: 47). Public and social monetary and banking systems are much older than markets, and certainly much older than metallic coins by thousands of years (Keynes 1971: 10). Early banking was based in institutions such as palaces and temples where monetary calculations took place in the recording of accounts. As Graeber points out, money throughout its history has been concerned with debts and obligations, often associated with structures of power and violence: 'the real origins of money are to be found in crime and recompense, war and slavery, honour, debt and redemption' (2011: 19). For Polanyi, far from the alleged benign origins in barter, market economies were developed by the activities of pirates, rovers, explorers and sword-bearing merchants (1944/57: 15). Graeber shares this view of 'impersonal markets, born of war, in which it was possible to treat even neighbours as if they were strangers' (2011: 238).

The myths of barter and precious metal have left a long legacy in economic thinking, even when the lack of historical evidence is acknowledged. In particular, the myth that money is commercial in origin goes very deep and supports the claim that value and wealth can only be understood in terms of commercial judgements. The main legacy of the barter myth is that the functions of money are defined in relation to trade. In most economic textbooks the primary function of money is given as a medium of exchange. The assumption is that this is exchange for profit, money invested in a commodity to generate more money (M – C – M+). As has been argued earlier, this is not the only way money can be used; it could equally be used for the exchange of use value or public value. The fact that money did not originate in barter, but was used as the basis of social or public means of account and means of payment, is overcome in economic theories of money by *assuming* that the starting point in economic theorising is barter. For the myth peddlers, if reality does not fit the theory, the solution is to change reality by ignoring the real history of money in favour of *a priori* assumptions and models.

The Perils of Coinage

While many forms of money have existed across history and culture, Europe's long use of coinage has influenced western economic thinking. Precious metal coinage was invented long after banking, but over two thousand years before capitalism. It emerged around 600 BCE, in (at least) three separate places: present-day Turkey, India and China (Graeber 2011). The most significant aspect of the emergence of coinage was that it was not associated with trade but with political power. Coinage issue through history has been mainly dominated by rulers and authorities, not traders. Where traders did create coinage, it was usually under licence. As Huber argues, 'traditional coin currencies for about 2,500 years were created and issued debt-free by being spent rather than loaned into circulation by the rulers of the realm' (2014: 51). Evidence of the early use of coinage shows an important link between coinage and empire. The newly invented precious metal coinage was used by rulers mainly to establish and extend their power, often through the payment of mercenary soldiers. The classic example was Alexander the Great who, it is reputed, used half a ton of silver a day to fund his imperialist adventures (Davies 2002: 82). As Davies argues, 'after Alexander the power to coin money became more obviously, but not exclusively, a jealously guarded sovereign power, the first to be assumed by any conquering army' (2002: 83). Another aspect of the public nature of coinage is the role of coins as symbols of nationhood, which has a lineage going back to the use of images on coin by early Greek cities.

In many ways, the emergence of precious metal coinage was an aberration in the history of money. It brought a 'natural' limitation into the money system that led to vicious colonial invasions and widespread conflict. Spanish treasure ships from the New World were closely guarded by warships. Any less well protected merchant ships were harassed by official and unofficial pirates. The demand for precious metals led to a close connection between money, trade and militarism (Mellor 2014). The era of mercantilism was based on the calculation of a nation's wealth by its ownership of precious metal bullion and dominance in trade. The aim was to amass as much precious metal as possible, and use military support to establish trading monopolies and trading empires. European countries fought to safeguard trading posts and trade routes. A problem arose when areas of the world with desirable goods such as China refused to trade in return (nothing has changed in that regard). In the early nineteenth century, British silver piled up in China through its exports of silk, porcelain and tea. Britain retaliated by launching the Opium Wars to force China to continue to import Indian opium for payment in silver.

Alongside mercantilism, Europe was beginning the process of consolidation into what would become nation states. Disputed land was the basis of wars, fortifications and standing armies. This cost a lot of money and local rulers often borrowed from the emerging merchants and bankers if their money, tax receipts or precious metal holdings were not sufficient. Political power and economic power were thus entwined in the emergence of European banking. The early Italian bankers such as the Medici linked economic, military and political power. Rulers also repaid loans with privileges such as a trading monopoly. During the crusades, proto-banking networks such as the Knights Templar arranged the transport and international settlement of payments and debts en route. Similarly, the Rothschild banking empire was built during the Napoleonic wars. As will be argued in the next chapter, this interweaving of ruler privilege in the creation of money, and the provision of loans to the state by bankers, has created confusion about the status and role of public monetary authorities such as central banks.

The history of precious metal coinage has also supported the myth that public money must have its origin in something of intrinsic value. This received philosophical justification in Britain from classical liberalism. At the end of the seventeenth century campaigners led by John Locke demanded that coins be made only of precious metal. This would be 'real' money that could exist as a neutral medium of trade and separate money from political power. Other voices strongly advocated the alternative of nominal, face value money, arguing that money was in essence a political project (Desan 2014: 335). In the end both views prevailed. Locke provided the argument for what became the gold standard, while in practice money became increasingly based on paper. This has led to the myths, confusions and contradictions about money that exist today.

One of the reasons that the precious metal story of the origin of money is so strong is that historical evidence of the existence of coinage survives. Less tangible forms of money with no link to coinage disappear. If tally sticks had been made of durable material the history of European money might be very different.

Tally Sticks

While European rulers embraced the prerogative of minting coin, spending the proceeds and retrieving it through taxation, this had its problems. If metal was in short supply or taxation did not successfully retrieve the coins, the financial position could be dire. The irony of the demand that coins should contain precious metal was that the consequent shortages created the conditions for other forms of money to emerge. Much sovereign (and commercial) finance was carried out using a much cheaper monetary medium, notched wooden tallies: 'from time immemorial, scored or notched wooden sticks have been used in many parts of the world for recording messages of various kind, particularly payments' (Davies 2002: 148). Instead of coins, rulers paid their accounts through sticks marked with the amount agreed. The stick was then split down the middle and the supplier held one half and the ruler the other. Alternatively the ruler used a tally to acknowledge a tax paid in advance. As the tallies could not be counterfeited they were trusted and circulated. Most importantly they could be used in payment of taxes, or in proof of tax paid.

In Britain tallies were used from at least the twelfth century and by the medieval period 'a majority of public revenues paid to public creditors took the form of tallies' (Desan 2014: 172). Davies reports that the money supply in England and Wales in 1698 had coins at 43.6 per cent and tallies and other money forms such as bank notes and bills at 56.4 per cent (2002: 280). He notes that Adam Smith calculated that in 1707 the position in Scotland was 25 per cent coinage to 75 per cent paper money. Fiat paper money created on public authority alone was also extensively used elsewhere.

Public Paper Money

China was an early example of the use of paper money when a severe shortage of copper led to its introduction by the emperor Hien Tsung (806–21). Over time, the use of paper money became extensive. By 1032 there was a large amount circulating with several private issuers. In a pattern that was to be repeated elsewhere, many of the private issuers failed and private notes were outlawed. While paper money was widely used in China, attempts to spread it beyond China and the heart of the Mongolian empire were not successful (Davies 2002: 180–1).

The American colonies were another example of the use of paper to meet problems in establishing a money system. The early colonists were chronically short of coin and were prevented from setting up banks by Britain (Davies 2002: 462). Some interpretations of the Boston Tea Party argue that it was not a protest about taxation as much as the right to create and issue money in the colony. Solutions were found such as using the local money, wampum, strings of shell beads, that were made legal tender in Massachusetts in 1641. Tobacco was also declared legal tender in Virginia in 1642. Massachusetts Bay Colony 1690 is credited as the first to use paper money. Faced with soldiers needing to be paid, the colony's leaders gave them notes promising to exchange them for hard coin later. The colonists then began to use the notes more widely and eventually they were declared legal tender for the payment of taxes. Other states followed including South Carolina, Rhode Island, Pennsylvania, New York, New Jersey and Delaware. In all cases the notes were spent into existence, not lent by banks. Maryland paid a dividend to all taxable citizens and made funds available for loans to farmers and businesses. The success of the money in the various states depended on how carefully it was used and the relationship it had to the capacity of the economy.

In 1729 Benjamin Franklin proposed the introduction of a publicly authorised paper money in *A Modest Enquiry into the Nature and*

Necessity of a Paper Money. In 1766 he travelled to address the British House of Commons on the proposal. This was rejected, and the paper money experiments in America were banned. Galbraith sees this as a major trigger in the War of Independence. Far from obeying the British edict, colonial government notes were issued to fund the rebellion. According to Galbraith, between 1775 and 1779 notes worth more than $450 million were issued across the country as 'overwhelmingly the Revolution was paid for with paper money' (1975: 59). However, the failure to tax was a problem. The public money circuit was not completed, too much money was in circulation, prices rose and it had to be made a law to accept the paper money in payment. In the post-revolutionary period there was a return to coinage produced only by the government. This was suspended from 1812 to 1814 and then abandoned totally in the Civil War when both sides relied once again on paper money issue. The South based its money on cotton while the North created 45 billion 'greenback' dollars based upon nothing. This was the more sensible arrangement, as the South's system broke down when the North blockaded the export of cotton.

The French revolution also saw the introduction of paper money 'assignats'. They were issued on the promise that they would be redeemed in five years by sale of church and state lands. This promise was undermined by over-issue. Following the Russian revolution nearly all the budget was met by paper money. Paper money was not just a money to be adopted in revolutionary situations. By the end of the twentieth century across the world all pretence of any link of paper money with precious metal was abandoned. Before that, however, strenuous efforts were made to make the precious metal link a reality.

The Search for 'Sound' Money

The continuing myth of the origin of money in precious metal has led to a debate between those who stress the social and public nature of money and those for whom the gold story is a historical, or hypothetical, starting point. This debate sets the idea of 'sound money' against money as a token existing only by fiat (trust or authority). The latter view would see all forms of money as tokens representing social, public or commercial entitlements or obligations between people. Where standards of 'objective' value have been asserted such as the link to gold, these are established by public authorities, not by any intrinsic standards of value. The gold standard was not related to the intrinsic value of gold, but to the attachment of a particular money value to it at a particular point in time. The idea that this represented an 'invariant monetary standard' was a 'working fiction' (Ingham 2004: 144). As Desan points out, the gold standard was not a 'free standing' value, it was part of domestic monetary policy. Even deciding on a price for gold depended on the pre-existence of coined money (2014: 409).

The link with money can be seen as stabilising the price of gold rather than gold stabilising the value of money. Since de-linking, the gold price has fluctuated wildly (Swift 2014: 14). From 1970 to the early 1980s it went from $200 to nearly $2,000. In the early 2000s it slumped to $350 before rising again to $1,800 following the crisis. Only about a quarter of gold now goes to bullion, mostly held by the Fed in its vaults under Manhattan. Nearly 50 per cent is used in jewellery where enough gold to make a ring creates 20 tons of waste and uses dangerous chemicals such as cyanide. Around 10 per cent goes to coins and medals, mainly for investment or ceremonial use (Swift 2014: 16). As Keynes argued, gold is an 'archaic relic' that needs to be left behind.

The case against money being based on an intrinsic value was emphasised by the work of Mitchell Innes. In 1913/14 he published two articles in a banking journal that challenged the idea that trade relied on the actual value of precious metal coinage (Innes 1913). He argued that the functional value of the coin was more important than the actual value. The relative unimportance of the value of the actual coin was indicated by the use of the old Roman currency for calculation in much of Europe although there were none of the coins in circulation after the collapse of the Roman Empire. Equally the pound sterling never existed as a silver coin and the British guinea continued to be used as an expression of value long after the coin disappeared. As pointed out earlier, debased money was of much more practical use than restricting the issue of coinage to reserves of scarce precious metal. Purity of coinage often meant there was not enough coin to do business. Also, coins with high intrinsic value were often hoarded or melted down for their bullion value. As a result, countries which experienced the greatest economic growth were those whose leaders had 'indulged in the most severe debasement of their coinage' (Davies 2002: 647).

If the search for gold as the basis of 'sound money' is a chimera, the soundness of money must be found elsewhere: in its social and public foundations. Whatever form it takes, money exists within a money system. It is a token representing a notional value that is universally accepted and can be readily transferred between members of the monetary community. In the case of the dollar and other global currencies, the monetary community extends beyond the boundaries of the relevant monetary authorities. What matters is that people agree to honour the value that the money represents. Holding money in one form or another is a claim or entitlement that other members of the provisioning system agree to honour. For Ingham, money is 'a socially (including politically) constructed promise ... money is always an abstract claim or credit'; 'Moneyness' is provided by whatever is agreed as 'money of account' (2004: 198). All money is therefore a credit that can command resources based on whatever value it represents (Wray 2004: 234).

Rejection of the myth of the intrinsic value of money means that the search for 'sound money' cannot be directed at the money form itself. Instead, 'sound money' can only be a product of a 'sound' society, not of the 'natural' value of some scarce commodity. Confidence in money is confidence in the provisioning capacity of a society. People's trust in money reflects a trust in the society, organisations and authorities that create and circulate it – other people, traders, the banks and the state. Money as a social phenomenon does not just emerge spontaneously in society as the barter-commodity money theorists assumed; it has to be created and accepted in circulation. Money needs to be 'nurtured'. The danger of the myths around money is that seeing it as only circulating through the commercial circuit with its origins in debt threatens to undermine trust in money itself.

The history of money shows that the tenets of neoliberalism and handbag economics rest on false assumptions about the nature of money. These false assumptions extend to the relationship between money and banking. In particular, the myth that banks are just intermediaries between savers and borrowers. That they do not, themselves, create the public currency.

Myth 4: What do Banks do?

The myth of banking is that bank loans are based upon deposits, and banks merely provide a link between savers and borrowers. This rests upon a precious metal 'history': that bank deposits originated in the need to have a safe place to store precious metal coin. Unfortunately, this ignores the two thousand year history of banking before the use of metal coin and the role of rulers and elite institutions. Early banking was very much a state administered activity, originating in the centralisation of the grain harvest in Egypt and Mesopotamia (Davies 2002: 52). Accounts were kept of deposits and transfers for private and public payments. As Davies points out, grain acted as a quasi-money in Egypt for many centuries without being a 'precious' commodity (2002: 53). Private relations of credit and debt also emerged before coinage, requiring the first recorded publicly formulated banking code, the Code of Hammurabi, promulgated in Babylon between 1792 and 1750 BCE.

The assumption that precious metal money emerged before banking leads to the priority given to the role of depositors rather than lenders in the myth of banking. This leads to a distinction between 'real money' deposits and bank-issued 'credit money'. In the conventional bank story, it is a source of 'real' money such as gold that lies behind the emergence of non-precious sources of money such as paper. The story goes that precious metal money was not much use to the owner stored in vaults. However, using it was cumbersome and risked robbery. The solution was to use evidence of their valuable deposits in trade. If there was sufficient trust in the depositor and the bank, third parties would accept the evidence of the deposit in payment. Banks would then either pay 'real' money out to the third party or adjust the relative deposits of the two parties in the clearing process. This remains a central aspect of the role of banks today: the settling of payments through bank transfers via a 'clearing' process within and between banks. The more the exchanges can be sorted out via accounting the less use there is for any medium of final payment. The idea that the ultimate form of settlement has intrinsic value makes this arrangement seem straightforward, a transfer of 'real money' is the end of the process. However, if money is seen as a social medium without intrinsic value, what is being transferred, and how a final payment can be achieved, is less clear, as is the source of bank deposits.

If the myth that banks link savers and borrowers were correct, at its most basic, the bank would lend someone's deposit with their permission to a third party. For a fee and interest the bank would take the risk that the loan would not be paid back. The money would either be in the bank or be lent out. If the money is lent, the depositor cannot have it back: gold cannot be in two places at once. However, according to the myth banks get around this problem by making a loan that is a representation of that deposit. Two representations may therefore exist, the note held by the depositor and the note held by the borrower. It is this that has led to the accusations of cheating. There is no direct relationship between the depositor and the borrower, nor is there assumed to be permission on the part of the depositor. Rather the bank is seen as establishing a broad, and seemingly dishonest relationship between deposits and loans.

This is the murky world of fractional reserve banking where bankers are seen as lending almost all of the deposits, or multiples of the deposits, despite the fact that the depositors could come back for them at any time. Only a fractional reserve is held on the assumption that the depositors would not all come back at once. What then are banks actually issuing when they make loans? The idea that banks hold a fractional reserve implies that they are lending out actual deposits of some tangible form of money or some promise related to those deposits. A distinction is then made between two types of money: the deposit 'real money' and the bank-issued 'credit money'. With a nod back to the link of money with gold, this 'real money' is seen as identified with the state. This notion of public 'real money', high powered money or base money, will be discussed in the next chapter. Here, however, we can note the irony that a theory of 'real' money that originated with classical liberalism has to invoke money from the state, while its progeny neoliberalism denies there is such a thing as public money.

Banks as Promises

The picture is very different if banking is not seen as evolving from fractional reserves of precious metal coinage, but from a less tangible world of promises and credit. Unlike gold, promises can be in two places at once. This alternative conception stems from the long history of bonds, credit and discounting that forms the basis of commercial banking. Far from requiring caches of precious metal, much early bank business was conducted on promissory notes and bills of exchange. The 'wealth' of the bank was not based on misusing depositor's money, but on the assets and reputation of the banker. Well-regarded bankers would act as a trusted intermediary, not between bank depositors and borrowers, but between debtors and creditors. They were not taking in hard forms of money and lending it out, or notes based upon it, they were taking in less creditworthy promises and putting their own credibility in its place.

For example, if a trader had no form of money to pay a supplier she or he could make a promise to pay with the proceeds of a future trade. However, the trader's promise would not carry very much weight, so the supplier might take it to a banker who had a reputation for cred-itworthiness based on personal wealth (or the illusion of wealth), and ask for a credit note from the banker for a lesser (discounted) value than the trader's promise. The banker would then take the risk of receiving the full payment from the trader in due course. This form of banking was not conducting fractional reserve banking based on deposits, but it was engaging in multiple representations of the banker's own creditworthiness. From this perspective, the issue of promissory notes and bills of exchange were the origin of modern commercial money, not ruler-dominated precious metal coinage. This use of 'elastic' credit can be seen as a critical development in the emergence of capitalism (Ingham 2004: 115).

Confusion about the nature of banking, whether it represents credit based on deposits of 'sound money' or relies on the capital wealth of the bank in the production of new credit, goes to the heart of the fragility of banking today. Banks certainly hold deposits, but as will be discussed below, most of these originate from the banking sector itself, as loans. Banks do hold assets including bank capital, cash reserves and future (re)payments from outstanding loans, but these are too little or too long term as against their liability to provide money on demand to all those who hold bank accounts. In practice, no bank can withstand a run. They are always illiquid in terms of cash (public currency notes and coin and reserves at the central bank) and in crisis situations insolvent, as most banks do not have sufficient assets to back more than a small proportion of bad loans. Modern banking is always caught in the trap of having short-term liabilities to its account holders and long-term exposure on its lending. In the run up to the 2007–8 crisis, banks operated on very little capital, by some calculations less than 1 per cent (D'Arista 2008). Even after the crisis, regulators were still envisaging only around 3 per cent capital ratios. It is clear from such low figures that it would never be expected that banks would rely on their own 'backing' for all but the most limited adverse conditions. Implicitly or explicitly they were relying on the state.

As the crisis showed, support was not just limited to state-backed deposit insurance for high street 'retail' banks. It spread much more widely, as even investment banks and investment activities needed to be supported. Central banks poured out money as lender of last resort when the assets of banks proved insufficient. What is critical to the argument of this book is the point at which bank accounts based on bank loans became designated as public currency. Once designated as public currency, the security of bank deposits became a responsibility of the public sector.

Banks Create Public Currency

Like the view that money had its origins in precious metal coinage emerging out of barter, the precious metal story about how banks issue money has a grain of truth, but creates a false picture. The general assumption that when someone puts a deposit in the bank it becomes the basis of fractional reserve banking relies on there being an external (exogenous) source of deposits. This leads to the claim that there are two forms of money: one that Keynes called 'money proper' (1971: 5) and another inferior 'credit money' issued by banks. Theories of fractional reserve banking then go on to argue that banks build upon the money proper (taken to be precious metal coinage or publicly authorised money) to create a 'multiplier' level of borrowing. A requirement on banks to keep 'credit money' in a fixed ratio to 'money proper' would be a constraint on the multiplier.

As pointed out earlier, the irony of handbag economics' denial of the ability of the public sector to create money is that it seems to provide no basis for the existence of 'money proper' that the banking myth requires. If there are to be 'prior' depositors before lending can begin, where do those deposits come from? In the absence of precious metal, the only possible external source of bank deposits is the public sector's capacity to create money. In short, for the myth of banking to stand, the public sector must mint coins, 'print money' or issue electronic money. This is precisely what handbag economics says it must not do. Failure to acknowledge this leads to a contradiction where conventional economics clings to the idea of 'real money' but has no theory of where it comes from. That leaves no source for bank deposits other than the banking sector itself. One way in which conventional economics circumvents the problem of money creation is to assume that a stock of money already exists. The analysis is then limited to the circulation of existing money, rather than the need to have a theory of the origin of new money.

The conventional 'exogenous' theory of the link between 'real' public currency and bank-created 'credit money' is challenged by 'endogenous' theorists who claim that the presumed relationship between public and private money does not exist. Public money does not drive private money; privately created money is in control. As Keynes argued: 'far from the actively created deposits being the offspring of the passively created deposits it is the other way round' (1971: 22). Bank deposits are not based on some form of public 'money proper', but are the product of bank-created debt. 'Endogenous' theorists of money reject both the deposit and capital asset 'fractional reserve' view of the process of banking. Instead, they argue that banks are in the business of creating money when they lend. It is this money that forms the basis of bank deposits. New money is deposited by the bank itself in the form of a 'credit' in a bank account (as in a personal, mortgage or business loan). This is then spent by the borrower (as cash or in a bank transfer) and becomes a 'new' deposit in other people's accounts.

Even if people did deposit state-issued money in the bank, banks do not lend depositors' money in any direct sense. If they did, no one could withdraw their money until debts were repaid. In fact, people can withdraw their money from deposit accounts on demand. A bank loan is therefore not a transfer from depositors to borrowers, it is always the creation of new money. In Galbraith's often repeated words, 'the process by which banks create money is so simple that the mind is repelled. Where something so important is involved, a deeper mystery seems only decent' (1975: 18–19). Bank-issued money, like publicly issued money, is created out of thin air. Like the 'printed money' that handbag economics so derides, it is 'fountain pen money' (Tobin 1963: 408), or in modern terms, keystroke money.

Modern banking, and the capacity for the virtually unlimited creation of money through debt, has enabled capitalist expansion (Mellor 2010a: 107). For Ingham, 'the essence of capitalism lies in the elastic creation of money by means of readily transferable debt' (2004: 108). For Innes, 'if banks could not issue money they could not carry on their business' (1914: 53). As the commercial circuit demands, far from money representing prior market activities as the barter theorists claimed, it is the prior issuing of bank credit that is essential to bringing profit-seeking activities into being. It is not linking savers and borrowers but 'credit creation (that) is the actual business of banking' (Smithin 2009: 66). Loans must precede deposits as 'loans can never be financed by some pre-existing deposits' (Parguez and Seccareccia 2000: 106–7). This is because only credit (i.e. debt) can start the commercial money circuit. The flexibility of bank-issued money is that it is independent of deposits. Even writing in 1930 Keynes acknowledged that 'bank money' formed around nine-tenths of current money usage at that time (1971: 27).

The endogenous view of banking puts the impetus for money creation firmly in the hands of borrowers. The money supply is entirely driven by the borrowing of individuals, companies and governments. Banks have not been mediating between savers and borrowers or channelling 'idle money' to 'productive use', as conventional theory would suggest. Nor are they a benign third party easing credit relations between clients; they play an active role in credit creation and 'loan-pushing' that has broadened the money supply into the non-banking financial sectors (Ozgur and Erturk 2008: 14). As Erturk and Solari have described it, the main focus of lending in the run up to the crisis was 'finance feeding finance' (2007: 378).

High street banks were not only creating new money through loans to financial institutions but were themselves borrowing from other banks and the wider money markets to support large-scale speculative trading, once regulatory restrictions were removed. As will be shown in the next chapter, central banks have no choice but to support whatever scale of debt-based money creation the banks present, because all loans are created as public currency. When commercial banking originated, the credit issued represented private money. A bank note was just that: a note drawn on a particular bank. However, a big change occurred when banks stopped creating money based on their own wealth (which was sometimes virtually non-existent) and created money based on the wealth of the nation, that is, their notes were designated in the public currency.

Bank Profit: Public Responsibility

As the crisis has shown, the creation of the public currency as debt by banks is entirely out of the control of monetary authorities. As a result, economies lurch from being swamped in debt to credit crunches. As under handbag economics the aim is to reduce government borrowing to nil if possible, the creation of the public currency supply as debt rests entirely on the individual decisions of private borrowers and their personal preferences and commercial imperatives. There is no basis for a public view on those choices. The most important outcome of the dominance of bank-issued money is that the supply of a nation's money is determined by private or commercial decisions, while the state retains responsibility for managing and supporting the system, as has become clear through the financial crisis. Banks will only lend if there is a good chance of getting a profitable return. People will only borrow if they think they have a viable business project or sufficient income to repay the loan.

However, banks and borrowers do not necessarily make a rational assessment of the economic context and this can lead to instability and crisis where finance becomes 'fragile' (Nesvetailova 2007). While the public within a money system collectively bears ultimate responsibility for the failures of the privatised money creation system, there is no direct public influence on the overall direction of how that finance is issued, invested or used. As Chick points out, 'money confers on those with authority to issue new money the power to pre-empt resources' (1992: 141). A privatised money supply, through a commercial banking structure, has no basis for democracy, other than the theoretical, but not actual, right of anyone to take out a loan.

Banks do not create debt-based public currency based on prior deposits or their own capital wealth but ultimately on the capacity of the people to provide goods, services and taxes. It would be possible to distinguish public money as 'money proper' from bank money if the two circuits of money were separate: if the state issued legal tender in the form of public currency, while banks issued credit notes upon themselves. The only thing 'backing' a bank in that event would be trust in its long-term viability. If most people honoured their debts the bank would survive and prosper. If they did not, it would fail, and many did. It is not possible to make this distinction when the two systems are intimately linked by the designation of bank deposits and notes as public currency. The problem with bringing the two money circuits together is that the public has become responsible for the integrity of the banking system. Far from issuing an inferior type of money, the banking sector has been issuing the national currency, albeit in accounting form. In this way, the supply of public currency has become privatised.

The dominance of the neoliberal ideology of 'market right, public wrong', means that the right of banks to issue the public currency for profit has not been challenged. The four myths still stand, although they are getting a bit tarnished. Given that, as Galbraith pointed out, bank credit is created out of thin air, like thin air it should arguably be seen as a public resource, even a 'commons' – a social resource in the same way that air or water is a natural resource (Mellor 2010a: 160). Given the public nature of money and the way its co-option by the financial sector has made the financial system a public liability, the logic is that such a public liability should also entail a public benefit. How money is issued and circulated then becomes a crucial social and political question. Given public liability, there would seem to be no case for the private ownership and control of the issue and circulation of the public currency. On the contrary, there would seem to be a strong case for the claim that public responsibility for the viability of national money should be accompanied by public discussion, that is, the money system should be a matter for democratic debate. Since all forms of money designated as public currency are a public liability, it should also be a public resource.

5

Janus-faced: The Central Bank

Janus is the Roman god of beginnings and endings, the month of January is named after him. Janus is also seen as guarding gates and doorways. The central bank can be seen as the gateway that connects the public and commercial circuits of money. However, in everyday use, Janus-faced also implies duplicity, and central banks face two ways: towards the public sector as represented by the state and public provisioning, and towards the commercial financial system as represented by the clearing banks, other financial institutions and the market. The direction that central banks favour determines the extent to which the supply of public currency is publicly or privately determined. For instance, quantitative easing could be used to channel new money into the financial sector, or be put directly into public hands as a citizens' disbursement, or be used for public benefit such as building hospitals or schools. The lesson from the crisis is that quantitative easing through the financial sector increases speculation and inequality.

Central banks are critical to modern monetary systems. Their role as a backstop in a crisis was clearly shown in 2007–8. It was not just that they created vast amounts of public money; they also had to convince the users of their public currency that it was valid and secure. Central to maintaining confidence was the authority behind the money. What, then, does the authority of central banks rely on and what is the money they are authorising?

Money in this book is defined as a readily accepted representation of a nominal unit of value that can be used to express actual obligations and entitlements. The money form itself can vary widely and may exist only as a verbal agreement or written record. Central to this definition of money is that the value is only representational. If the money form had a commodity value exactly equivalent to the object being valued, there would be no need for it to be supported by social trust or public authority. However, the history of money shows that money forms have very rarely matched nominal value to intrinsic value, even when composed of precious metal. In modern times, money economies have only resorted to using commodity forms such as tobacco or other products because of the absence of serviceable representational money. What the central bank is therefore securing is not the commodity value of money, but social trust in it based on public authority. Despite this, part of the history of central banking has involved the attempt to establish an intrinsic base for money such as the gold standard, which will be discussed in Chapter 7.

Central banks are at the heart of nominal public currency systems. They are the public monetary face which reflects social trust and monetary authority. Social trust is the belief that other people, even complete strangers, will honour the currency. Public trust is the perception that the money system is well managed and able to sustain the money supply. As the crisis has shown, central to support for the public currency and the commercial banking system is the capacity of central banks to create public money free of debt. The second thing the crisis has shown is that this capacity is not sufficient in itself. There also needs to be a thriving public circuit of money, including surplus expenditure where necessary. This is described by handbag economics as a deficit. The euro is unravelling because it was an attempt to create a public currency system based solely upon the commercial circuit of money. Currency could only be borrowed into existence by the banking system. With no public circuit there was no means of circulating new debt-free money through public expenditure or even direct public borrowing.

The history of central banks reflects the shifting relationship of the Janus-face pivot between their public and the private roles. The interconnected way they emerged has led to the confusion about the balance between these roles. Two main threads link the public and private aspects. One shifts from ruler to commerce, privatising money. The other shifts from private to public as privately issued promises became public currency.

The first thread starts from the historical assertion of rulers' control of monetary relations through the claim of sovereignty. This was a mixture of the exercise of outright power over resources, and the moral claim that the ruler was the embodiment of the state. Sovereign power endowed the privilege of seigniorage in relation to the creation of money. In this book that is taken to mean benefit of first use of that money, over and above the cost of creating it. Although both money and banking were developed and controlled by ruling elites wielding their tribute/taxation powers, they became captured by commercial actors as sovereign monetary power was waning. As discussed earlier, rulers needed more money than their authority and control of economic resources could obtain. As their ability to tax effectively declined, rulers had to turn to an alternative source of money by going into debt, using future tax income as collateral.

Rulers having to borrow money changed the public currency from being primarily an expression of power and/or authority to being a commodity for sale. However, this is a very different meaning of commodity money from the intrinsic value view of money. Money is not being valued because it is composed of a commodity (gold, silver). In privatised money systems, what is being sold is the belief – credit/credere – in a nominal money form. The money being borrowed was not primarily public currency as coin, it was a range of private promises and money forms. The newly emerging private banking system saw both a shift in the control of money away from the ruler and a move away from coinage. In the process, banks also took over the seigniorage powers of the sovereign: 'Banks can carry out on a large scale what was formerly the privilege of sovereign, that is, they purchase assets with their own bank money' (Huber 2014: 51).

The second thread starts from the capture of the ruler's prerogative by private banks. Although powerful banks took over the sovereign power to create money, this was not without its problems, as banks failed to honour the promises they had made. Central banks emerged to constrain the production of private money by imposing a centralised public money form. In this way central banks play a crucial role in the privatisation of the public currency by taking public responsibility for its viability. The interconnected public and private faces are reflected in the main functions of modern central banks. These include: securing the public currency in its various money forms (coins, notes, bank accounts etc.); overseeing overall management of the banking system; creating public money (sometimes shared with the Treasury); selling cash currency to banks on demand; acting as a clearing house for interbank activities; managing external currency relations; managing government accounts; lending to government and banks. The actual functions of individual central banks will depend on how these responsibilities are prioritised. Under neoliberal handbag economics the central bank is seen as having only one face: to support and stabilise the privatised monetary system. As the crisis shows, however, to do so requires the use of its public face.

Understanding the Confusion: The History of Central Banks

The Janus-faced nature of central banks reflects their varied origins. Over time, central banks have been set up in different ways: some were established as public institutions while others were, or are, private sector organisations. For example the US Federal Reserve structure, set up after a long conflict over the necessity for a central bank, remains a private sector organisation. Some central banks started out as private and became public, such as the Bank of England. More recently central banks have been generally established as part of the state apparatus. Central banks can also have different functions, or different emphases. For example, the origin of the Bank of England primarily as a banker to the state is very different from the European Central Bank set up at the height of neoliberal handbag economics to serve only the banking system. To understand the confusing role of central banks it is helpful to explore their history.

The two faces have evolved because modern central banks emerged out of elements of both the state monetary structure and the commercial banking system. They consolidated themselves over a long period. For example the Bank of England, founded in 1694 to finance the state, only took on the full monetary control powers of a central bank in 1844 and was not nationalised until 1946. Central banks also emerged out of the complex interaction of rulers and the increasingly powerful merchant class. In many cases rulers themselves were also bankers and merchants. For example the Medici family were bankers, rulers, even pawnbrokers. Banking families such as the Rothschilds performed many of the roles now associated with central banks, particularly lending to states and the clearing of cross-national banking payments.

Securing the Currency: The Bank of Amsterdam

Although coinage was the main early form of money in Europe, rulers were increasingly less able to exert the control that the early empires such as those of Alexander and the Romans had displayed. The invention of precious metal coinage was a huge boost to sovereign power, particularly in the payment of mercenaries, but it was also a weakness. Precious metal coinage had a paradoxical effect, as although it was very much a public institution, dominated by rulers, the rulers depended on access to the metal which was often in the hands of traders and adventurers. Traders brought bullion to be melted into coin for a fee. The balance of value between coin and bullion was delicate. There was always the danger that people would prefer to extract the precious metal from the currency if its commodity price went too high, causing a dramatic shortage of coinage. For this reason debased coin was often more useful. Most early coins did not have values on their faces, the value of each coin was announced by ruling authorities. This allowed rulers to 'cry up' or 'cry down' the value of their coinage. Needing to guarantee the value of metal coinage led to the formation of one of the first central banks, the Bank of Amsterdam. However, its history also shows the importance of non-coinage currency.

Amsterdam's public authorities created the Bank in 1609 as a joint stock bank. Amsterdam at the time was an international centre of commerce with a stock exchange functioning as early as 1585. As a result, a range of coins were in circulation, many of uncertain quality. Holland itself had two forms of coinage: high quality coins for external trade and more inferior coins for internal use. This points to a major difference between money operating within a social and public setting and intrinsic value money that could cross borders. Desan argues that only the former can strictly be defined as money: 'Money was a domestic affair, a political project based on the institutions of minting, spending, taxing, adjudicating, and enforcing that made it work as a way to count value, settle debts, and circulate at home. Stripped of that infrastructure – outside of the engineering that made it circulate as *money* – coin was, in fact, bullion' (2014: 347, italics in the original).

The Bank of Amsterdam enhanced the quality of the coinage by taking over the role of coinage minting from a range of private coiners. The Bank also provided deposit facilities for large-scale users of both internal and external coin and registered them as 'a credit in its books' (Davies 2002: 551). These credits were often more highly valued than the actual coins, which became damaged and tarnished. In 1668 the Bank of Sweden became the first central bank to issue bank notes that could be circulated as public currency.

Dutch currency in all its forms (coin and paper record) became the dollar of its day. However, the Bank of Amsterdam was an early warning of Minsky's instability thesis: a secure monetary base led to extreme levels of credit being created during the tulip mania of 1634–37. As Davies argues, it showed that 'the much admired financial sophistication of the Dutch could be carried to excess – a lesson almost every generation has subsequently needed to relearn for itself, ever since "bank money" greatly expanded man's ambitions' (2002: 553).

While the Bank of Amsterdam's main face was directed towards the need to secure the international commercial role of money, a second major role for the new national banks was to supply rulers with finance. Key to their Janus-faced structure, central banks combined two important tasks: lending to states, and guaranteeing the quality of the nation's public currency. In contemporary society this is interpreted as creating and managing the national debt and providing 'real money' to support the rest of the banking system in its creation of the bulk of the money supply as debt. The role of the central bank in the creation of public debt is clearly seen in the history of the Bank of England.

Financing Rulers: The Bank of England

The history of the Bank of England, like much of the relationship between rulers and lenders, was rooted in the expense of war. As has been argued earlier, the history of coinage is much more associated with war than trade. King William needed money to fight the French but the British monarchy had a bad credit rating resulting from earlier

Stuart defaults. Increasingly, the seventeenth century saw political limitations on the monarchical power to capture money or levy taxes (Goodman 2009: 10).

In 1694 a group of merchants led by William Paterson came together to provide the King with a loan of £1.2 million on which interest of 8 per cent per annum would be paid. The loan was composed mainly of credits: 'the Bank was a consortium of individuals who loaned the Crown money in the form of paper promises-to-pay' (Desan 2014: 14). On the security of Parliament's promise to repay the loans out of taxes another £1,200,000 in notes was created and lent to commercial borrowers. This met a growing commercial requirement for new money. Davies argues that the formation of the Bank of England was not just based on the needs of the state, but also on the needs of traders for cheap credit leading to 'a popular clamour for a public bank to compare with those of Italy, Sweden and especially Holland' (2002: 239). As Davies points out, in 1694 when the Bank of England was founded, there was equal lending to the state and the private sector. The two forms of loan, public and commercial, were closely connected. Credit notes issued to the private sector were secured on the Parliamentary guarantee to pay the debts of the sovereign. Paper money was needed because a bullion-based coinage would not be sufficient to represent the level of wealth and trade in the nation. Britain had expanding colonies and new luxury goods such as tea, coffee, sugar, tobacco and furs, but Spain had the gold. Even then, the gold that was available was not funding expansion in trade but raising prices. What was needed was a reliable and trusted source of credit rather than 'the jumble of goldsmiths, scriveners, merchant banks and other informal sources of money and credit' (Goodman 2009: 11). Coinage usage was already in relative decline. In 1697 when Parliament allowed the Bank of England to increase investment subscriptions by £1 million, 80 per cent of this was subscribed by tallies issued by the Crown, the rest in bank notes (Davies 2002: 262).

As the commercial sector had expanded, and particularly commercial banking, wealth had accumulated in the hands of the new commercial elite. This wealth took the form of assets, including coinage, but also commercial credit. The new plutocrats had sufficient wealth to support extensive lending. The Bank of England notes held particularly high status. Rather than taxing through creating its own money such as coin or tally sticks, the state was now borrowing the privately owned Bank's note money. Overall, the supply of bank-created money, composed of notes, bills and cheques, had exceeded coinage in Britain by the time of the publication of Adam Smith's *Wealth of Nations*, and 'the new forms of bank money brought a liberating, timely and essential extension to overcome the debilitating constraints of the metallic money supply' (Davies 2002: 239). As commercial credit expanded, private banks started to open accounts with the Bank of England and use its notes. For Galbraith, the Bank of England is to money what St Peter is to the Faith (1975: 30). However, Bank of England notes could still be redeemed in coin until 1797 when wars with the French led to the suspension of conversion until 1821. This on-off relationship with bullion continued until the final abandonment of the gold standard in Britain in 1931.

The formation of the Bank of England was politically contentious. Land-owning Tories opposed its formation because it would strengthen the protestant King and Parliament against the aristocratic landowners, many of whom wanted to re-establish the House of Stuart (Goodman 2009: 18). Tories also argued that banks were republican by nature, while Whigs thought loans to the Crown would strengthen the King against Parliament by providing an alternative source of money. The Whigs thus added a clause saying the King could not borrow without permission (Galbraith 1975: 32). Merchants opposed the establishment of the Bank of England because they thought it would raise interest rates and monopolise the country's money. They posted an amendment that the Bank could not engage in trade in goods (Goodman 2009: 19). These pressures, however, were as nothing compared to the politics of the American Central Bank.

The Fed

The Federal Reserve system in the US did not emerge from a long history of coinage or autocratic rulers. Nor did it arise out of ancient customs in money or banking. There was no need to transfer monetary creation powers from a ruler once independence from Britain had been established. Although the US developed as a market society with a neoliberal philosophy of rugged individualism and limited governance from its inception, it also has a public history including the creation of state paper money. While the Constitution explicitly granted the right to create coined money to Congress (Article I, Section 8, Clause 5), the position for paper money was less clear.

Starting as a new democracy the US was building its monetary and banking system as it built its state(s). 'In no other country ... has the subject of money and banking given rise to such long-sustained, deep-rooted, widespread, acrimonious, publicly debated and eagerly reported controversy as in America' (Davies 2002: 473). State-created paper money funded the war of independence from 1775 to the early 1780s, but over-issue meant that faith in the currency began to be undermined (Blain 2014: 76–7). A Bank of North America (BNA) was proposed that would put private money in place of public money. Founded in 1782 the bank operated on paper money just like the federal greenbacks, but had the mystique of the promise of private capital.

Bob Blain has translated into modern language a debate in 1786 about the relative merits of publicly and privately created money in the Pennsylvania General Assembly (personal communication). It took place because the BNA had had its charter rescinded and was campaigning to have the decision overturned. The main thrust of the case for the BNA was that once a charter had been granted to a bank by an elected assembly it was unjust for a second assembly to overturn the decision because of the economic repercussions for the stockholders in the bank. Further arguments were that commercial banking produced liberty and prosperity because 'every man' could 'pursue his own benefit in his own way'. Evidence was cited of how commercial banking had expanded trade in Europe.

The case against the bank argued that its supporters were acting from private interest rather than in the public interest. The point in contention was who had the right to 'emit money'. The existing position where the state had been creating and lending paper money for 40 years with 'utmost utility' would be undermined. Instead of earning interest, the state would end up paying interest. To renew the charter would give the bank the privilege of creating money with no benefit to the state. Rather it would 'injure our country', being 'incompatible with public welfare'. It might even worsen the balance of trade through encouraging imports. The bank could also undermine commercial competition by giving advances of money to 'their particular favourites'. The evidence from Europe, it was argued, indicated that banks had a tendency to accumulate wealth in the hands of the bank stockholders. The BNA had earned profits of more than 16 per cent a year, but this just encouraged investment in further lending rather than in actual production such as housing or agriculture. The opponents of the BNA won the debate and state control of money continued. The BNA eventually got a charter from Delaware and subsequently became part of Wells Fargo.

One interesting resonance with the current crisis is the way the public sees a publicly chartered bank. Unpaid soldiers were threatening to loot the BNA in June 1783 on the grounds that a government-chartered bank should be responsible for the payment of government debts (Davies 2002: 473). In the current crisis the position was reversed and the state was expected to honour the monetary liabilities of state-licensed private banks.

Blain points out that the supporters of the BNA went on to clear the way for the privatisation of the money supply by denying Congress the power to create paper money in the Constitution, which only mentions coinage (for which at that time metal was in short supply). The new Congress also had to take responsibility for all the war debts which speculators were busy buying up at huge discounts. Like debt vultures today, they pressed for the full payment. Having lost the monopoly on producing paper money, Congress was forced to borrow bank-issued paper money and begin the build-up of the national debt. The national money supply as a whole became increasingly based on debt. Blain points out that from 1781 onwards, public and private debt grew in an almost a straight line at the rate of nearly 8 per cent per year. This was much faster than other socioeconomic indicators. From 1916 to 2012 the US population grew threefold, inflation went up by 22 times, GDP grew 155 times but total debt expanded by 907 times (Blain 2014: 72).

As banks sprang up across the US, the aim seems to have been to restrict their power by keeping them local, confined within state boundaries, rather than regulating them at federal level. However this did not stop problems of over-indebtedness, particularly of farmers, and fragility of bank solvency. Without a central bank there was an unregulated free-for-all and many banks collapsed. There was one more failed attempt to set up a national bank before the Fed was finally established in 1913 in response to the crisis of 1907. That crisis was caused by a panic that began in the stock market but caused a run on a number of banks that were thought to have lent on the loss-making investments. The panic was stopped by J.P. Morgan, whose creditworthiness was sufficient to give people confidence to trust their banks.

The Fed is a private organisation representing the banking sector. Its commercial face is to provide 'liquidity', i.e. public money, to the banking system. Its more public face is that it must aim to maintain full employment, albeit via the commercial circuit. It is this more social role that enabled the Fed to take a much more Keynesian approach to the crisis than the neoliberal UK and Eurozone. However, according to Robert Poteat of the American Monetary Institute, the public lending the Fed has undertaken has 'been almost entirely devoted to funding US military adventures across the globe'. As a 'private banking cartel' the Fed's main role, says Poteat, is as a commercial backstop for commercially issued debt. This puts the nation's credit in place of that of commercial banks. He sees this as a form of laundering of commercially created money, turning privatised money supply into public money supply and private liability into public liability. Poteat points out that since the passage of the Act setting up the Fed, there have been 19 recessions in the US, including two major depressions, despite the Fed's responsibility for banking supervision (unpublished communication). A more recent example of a central bank with only a commercial face that has failed to prevent a crisis is the ECB.

ECB – The One-Faced Bank

> The ECB does not act as a genuine central bank since it supports banks within the eurozone, but lacks power to extend support to member states.
>
> (Lapavitsas et al. 2012: 56)

Writing in 1975 Galbraith argued that although the Federal Reserve was a private organisation, like all central banks it was kept on a tight leash by governments (1975: 30). Speaking of central banks generally, he observed that 'warring governments would ... turn to their central banks for the money that they could not raise in taxes ... no bank, whatever its pretence to independence, would even think of resisting ... it was the instrument of a ruling class' (Galbraith 1975: 43). This conception is a world away from the neoliberal insistence on central bank independence and the denial of ready access of governments to public money. The structure and remit of the Frankfurt-based European Central Bank specifically denies Eurozone governments direct access to the Bank. While commercial banks in the Eurozone have a common interest rate at which they can access public currency from the ECB, states are thrust on to the 'money markets', facing different borrowing rates depending on their commercially determined credit rating.

While commercial banks have effectively as much 'liquidity', i.e. ECB-generated public currency, as they want, states are entirely dependent on market forces. This does not affect the public money circuit, as Eurozone national central banks still manage state accounts and the circuit of expenditure and taxation. The problem comes with funding surplus expenditure (the deficit) and existing national debts. In countries with more traditional arrangements like Britain, the central bank holds and manages the national debt and can, if necessary, continue to hold the debt if the market fails to buy it. In the last resort it can 'print money'. This, Eurozone central banks cannot do.

According to Eurozone rules, the central bank cannot buy state debt directly, that is, the ECB cannot create money for that purpose. Instead, it must create and issue public money only to the commercial sector as a commercial loan. Commercial banks can then use that money to buy state debt. For this to make commercial sense, banks must borrow money from the ECB at a lower rate than they charge states. States, on the other hand, must pay much more than necessary for their borrowing. Financing states only by commercial debt means that money is constantly moving from taxpayers to the financial sector in interest and repayments. The financiers get richer and the general public (taxpayer) gets poorer. Many banks in the more prosperous euro countries had lent extensively to the governments of weaker countries. The bailout was as much for their benefit, and the mainly American banks that had insured against sovereign default.

Some commentators have seen the euro, with its fixed and limited approach to money, as an attempt to recreate the gold standard. This removes control of monetary management from individual countries. There is no longer a flexible central bank to help countries manage their debts and finance their budgets. Palley makes the case for Eurobonds, so that public debts become a shared obligation of all Eurozone governments. The inequality between Eurozone states also needs to be addressed. Germany should put the needs of the Eurozone before its own competitive advantage: 'Germany must shift to a domestic demand-led growth model based on rising wages so that it can play its proper role of locomotive for the larger European economy' (Palley 2013a: 11). As Colignatus (2013) argues, money should not be like gold, scarce and rigid. It should be like water, fluid and flexible. To solve the problems of the Eurozone he recommends that the ECB should create 800 billion euros. Half would be given to the banks, but 'sterilised', that is removed from circulation, by requiring a 10.5 per cent reserve. The rest would bail out the most indebted countries directly. This would recapitalise the banks and redress the injustice done by signing up countries to the euro when it was patently unsuitable for them.

The Eurozone's rigid approach to money creation was understandable in the light of the German hyperinflation experience. This led to the focus on 'profligate states' while at the same time ignoring the huge rise in the commercial money supply. Neither was action taken to counter the collapse in money supply that followed the crisis. The German obsession with an anti-inflationary strategy meant that most of the ECB remedies, such as the Securities Markets Program that bought up commercial bonds, were 'sterilised' by asking banks to deposit equivalent funds. This meant that bank balance sheets were cleaned up, but there was little relief for individuals, companies or governments. As a recent IMF paper argues, there has been a misreading of the German experience. The German state did not 'print money' during the hyperinflation, because the German banking system was in private hands at the time. The allies had insisted on private control of the Reichsbank in 1922. The new ownership allowed a massive expansion of private bank money to be exchangeable for Reichsmarks. Reichsmark loans were also readily available and there was open exchange with other currencies, resulting in high levels of speculation. Compounded by external pressure to make reparations, the monetary system collapsed. Hyperinflation was brought under control when a new central bank regime curtailed such flexible arrangements, a new public currency was created, and pressure for reparation eased (Benes and Kumhof 2012).

The 2007–8 crisis has fundamentally challenged the one-faced approach of the ECB. For five years it stood by its neoliberal principles, but in July 2012 Mario Draghi, head of the ECB, responded to what seemed to be a desperate position by proposing to do 'whatever it takes' to preserve the euro. This declaration was enough to calm the situation until 2014 when deflation threatened. Rather than a concern about inflation being too high, now it had fallen too low, that is, below 2 per cent with 1 per cent as the danger zone. In June 2014 with only 0.2 per cent growth, Draghi reduced interest rates to 0.05 per cent and even introduced a form of demurrage, a penalty for holding money, by charging interest of 0.1 per cent on bank reserves. This was not enough, and by 2015 a tip into deflation forced it to finally adopt the strategy of quantitative easing. Reluctantly, the ECB was reclaiming its public face. The experience was proof that the private circuit of money cannot exist without a vibrant public circuit.

Facing the Banks: Central Bank as Servant or Master?

Whether it is a public or private institution, a central bank acts as a public monetary authority. Its role is critical in sustaining the supply of public currency and responding to the needs of the wider banking system. Their role was crucial following the financial crisis as they created sufficient liquidity to rescue a banking sector that was largely insolvent. The central bank is deposit holder and clearing bank to the banks and 'lender of last resort'. How the relation between central banks and the banking sector is perceived depends upon the theory of money adopted. If it is assumed that money originally had an intrinsic value then a distinction is made between real money (high powered money, base money) and bank-issued 'credit money' (i.e. debt). Real money is the original source of monetary value and it is deposits and reserves of this money held by the central bank that backs the banks' creation of credit money. It holds that there is a relation between the amount of credit money the banks can lend and the reserve money they hold. The theory of fractional reserve banking that derives from this sees central bank control of reserves as key to its control over bank lending. By manipulating the amount of reserves demanded to be held, central banks can regulate the level of bank lending.

This assumes a multiplier ratio between reserves held and bank lending. A certain amount of reserves will trigger a certain multiple of lending. Other weapons in the central banks' armoury include the setting of base interest rates upon which other interest rates are calculated. The bank rate (base rate) is the rate at which the central bank would take in commercial bank assets in exchange for cash or the rate it would charge to lend money. Interest rates can also be manipulated by buying and selling government debt. All of these assumptions have been challenged following the crisis. Control of interest rates proved useless in face of commercial pressures. When central banks cut interest rates to the bone, commercial rates did not respond. Previous monetarist experiments in controlling the commercial money supply in order to reduce inflation were equally ineffective. The monetarist policies of making money more expensive through high interest rates did not reduce money supply or cut consumer spending but drove up the value of the currency, making imports cheaper and exports more expensive. This had a dire effect on export industries but fostered the growth of the financial sector, particularly as the monetarist experiment was accompanied by the neoliberal deregulation of the financial markets.

As Keynes predicted, there were limits to the ability of central banks to get commercial banks to lend. Following the crisis, money has been virtually thrown at the banking sector. Despite central bank loans being almost free and the launch of various schemes to encourage lending including quantitative easing, most of the money found its way back into bank reserves. What limited lending there was mainly fed financial speculation or mortgages. By early 2013, US commercial banks were sitting on massive, historically unprecedented reserves of $1.8 trillion, equivalent to more than 11 per cent of US GDP. Although cash reserves before the 2007–8 crisis were far too low, Robert Pollin argues that a reserve fund of $600 billion would be sufficient, leaving about $1.2 trillion that could fund productive loans (Pollin 2013: 64). The lack of success in getting banks to lend after the crisis was mirrored by the total failure to control them before the crisis.

The conventional view that central banks can control the amount that banks lend by manipulating reserves and interest rates has been widely challenged. As Lavoie points out, 'lending officers do not make their lending decisions after checking the reserve position of their bank at the central bank' (2010: 17). Steve Keen has also long argued that the money multiplier theory is a myth. There is no controlling link between the level of central bank reserves and the amount of commercial bank lending. Keen predicted the 2007–8 crisis on the evidence of huge increases in private debt. He argues that, far from controlling bank-issued debt, central banks increase the reserves available to match bank lending. Drawing on Australian evidence he shows that 'credit money was created first, and fiat money was then created about a year later' (2009b: 4).

Bank-created debt (the commercial money circuit often described as 'endogenous money') comes first and public money (central bank money, 'exogenous money') is created in reaction to the demands of the commercial banks. Central banks have no choice but to respond to demands for 'high powered money', and in the last resort provide new money to rescue the debt-loaded system. In any case, banks do not in the first instance borrow from the central bank. They settle their accounts through the central bank clearing facility and issue overnight loans to each other to cover any shortfall. The rate for these loans is the (much manipulated) LIBOR (London Interbank Borrowing Rate), which infamously broke free of any relation to the central bank rate in the run up to the crisis. The rate was set at four o'clock each afternoon through a survey of rates at which banks thought they could borrow at that time. During the crisis banks tended to under-report the rate as they did not want to alert other banks to their vulnerability. The assumption that there should be a powerful public control mechanism for the money system seems at odds with laissez faire neoliberal handbag economics and its 'household' view of the public sector. The contradiction is obscured by the assertion that central banks should be 'independent'. It was more radical economists who recognised the danger of the uncontrolled role of privatised money in capitalist economies. This may answer the British Queen's question as to why conventional economists did not 'notice it' coming. In the run up to the financial crisis they did not see the vast increase in the supply of privatised money as inflationary and speculative. This was because the main beneficiaries were those holding financial assets. Inflation in this context was celebrated as 'capital growth'. The dramatic expansion in the relationship of money supply to GDP was ignored.

Countries had levels of debt and speculative money well beyond the goods, resources and investment opportunities available. At least five times greater in the UK and ten times or more in Iceland. Much of this was built up by banks lending to each other: 'banks have simply been lending increasing amounts to each other as the financial sector has engaged in massive "proprietary trading" and gambling as they have tried to build up their income and bonus pools for their traders' (Epstein 2013: 91–92). Despite the crisis, by the end of 2013 the top banks in the US were even bigger as a proportion of GDP and still borrowing in the short-term and overnight markets. Levels of leverage had barely come down. With a legal requirement for equity capital of only 3 per cent, this meant banks could still borrow and lend up to 33 times that amount (Taub 2013: 106). The private money creating debt machine was still in full swing. As this book has argued, the money they are creating is not private, it is the public currency. This makes it a public responsibility. The private circuit of money cannot exist without 'high powered money'.

What is High Powered Money?

Writing in an era when most people still used cash (notes and coin), Galbraith argued that central banks provided 'a reliable supply of wholly acceptable money when ... people wished to turn their deposits in the commercial banks into the cash which, by the nature of deposit creation, was not there' (1975: 40). Such 'backing' for bank-created money was essential because 'the monetary achievement of the nineteenth century was a fragile thing' subject to a number of crises (Galbraith 1975: 42). What is this 'wholly acceptable money'? The illusion that it is gold has gone, and fewer people use cash, so what exactly are central banks providing?

In conventional money theory, high powered money (HPM) or base money refers to the money controlled by the monetary authority, usually seen as the total of bank reserves and cash in circulation. HPM is contrasted with credit money, the money created only as bank 'sight accounts', that is, existing only as a bank record. If an account holder asks for that record to be turned into cash, the bank has to buy this from the central bank paying from its reserves. Keynes saw bank money as 'acknowledgements of debt' whereas only HPM, 'money proper', could finally settle that debt (1971: 5–6). However, in practice, bank transfers between people are perfectly adequate in settlement of debt. Banks also settle debts between themselves at the level of the central bank, but it is not clear that they are using a special type of money to do so.

Distinguishing 'money proper' from bank money implies that bank-created money is a different form of money to state-created money. This was more clearly the case when bank notes were private agreements between borrowers, creditors and the bank and the only backing for the notes was trust in the long-term viability of the particular bank. With the establishment of public currencies, however, the right of banks to issue their own bank notes was largely prohibited. Banks could only borrow and lend central bank notes or produce their own notes by agreement. Theoretically, the central bank could now control lending through control of the amount of notes issued. Banks would only be able to act as a link between depositors and borrowers of the public currency as stated by the myth discussed earlier. However, limiting the number of bank notes in circulation did not limit the bank's ability to create 'sight accounts' designated in the public currency. Bank transfers could operate through paper or electronic records, as they increasingly do so today. For this reason this book describes bank records as public currency. Electronic records are as trusted as cash.

This is why central banks had to rescue their banks with unlimited support. All money created by the banks had to be backed by the state (Konings 2009, Montgomerie and Williams 2009). The ability of central banks to control sight accounts was an illusion. During the crisis a major concern was that ATM machines would run out of cash within minutes as there was so little in circulation compared with the sums held in bank accounts. The huge public declaration of state backing for the banks prevented what could have been an irreversible panic when people realised there was no 'real' money. States had to rescue their financial systems because they are responsible for the integrity of the national currency, while having little control over the day to day issue and circulation of money as bank debt. If bank credit wasn't 'real money' why did states feel compelled to underwrite their banking systems which, in Keynes' terms, will be riddled with private bank debt rather than 'money proper'? This answer is that the bank-created debt is the public currency. The public currency has been privatised as debt. Neither the state nor the people distinguish between different kinds of money. Cash and bank accounts can both be used in settlement of debt including taxes.

A lot of the confusion is caused by the myth of 'hard money'. If high powered money is taken to be the equivalent of gold there must be something tangible in reserve. However, precious metal was only ever available in relatively small quantities, compared to the total money in circulation, and other forms such as tally sticks and paper were widely used. Today public currency can be created both publicly and privately as electronic credits. The difference therefore cannot be one of form. In the two monetary circuits, public and commercial, money is designated as national tender. In both circuits money mainly exists in electronic form. Equally, there is little difference in the capacity of public and private money suppliers to cause inflation or deflation. The state can overtax or overspend. Banks can over-lend fuelling an orgy of speculation while a loss of confidence can bring a credit crunch.

However, there is still one clear point of difference between the state and the banking system as a source of money supply. The state can issue money without debt, whereas the profit-based capitalist banking system cannot. That is why the latter has an endemic tendency to crisis. There comes a point at which the circuit can take no more debt. At this point the money supply must turn to public money, public currency, publicly created. This is the crux of HPM. Only the state can stabilise the financial situation by creating money free of debt that has public authority and social trust. In the contemporary privatised money supply system the distinction between high powered money and 'bank money' is not helpful. All money is supplied as national tender and has to be backed by the state. The high power the state holds is the capacity of the state or monetary authority to give its money and financial system credibility and issue money free of debt. Ultimately what 'backs' the money is the willingness of the public to accept it in circulation. It is a combination of social trust and public authority.

Without this structure of state-based finance, capitalism cannot operate. In a crisis the state must step in. Not because the money it issues is 'high powered' as a medium, but because its role as a monetary authority is unique. As Ingham points out, 'the state and the market share in the production of capitalist credit money' (2004: 144). However, in the last resort, it is the state that is the most important. The elastic creation of bank-created 'credit money' is secured by the state's total liability for the system. Under handbag economics this means private benefit, but public responsibility. The commercial circuit is not private at all. It requires regular top ups from the public circuit. It is parasitic on the public capacity to create money free of debt. For this reason all creation of new money, whether by central banks or high street banks, is a public question, because it has implications for the public as a whole.

Money Captured: Sovereign Debt

The history of central banks shows that the creation of a national debt is closely aligned with the privatisation of the creation of the money supply to fund that debt. The Bank of England did not fund the King with gold or goods and services, they funded him with new paper promises and the cancellation of old crown debts. In the process taxation of the rich became replaced with borrowing from the rich. The National Debt was born. Over time, the private paper promises became the public currency and central banks developed their two faces. They are issuing public money which is free of debt at the point of creation, reflecting the sovereign right to create money, but it is then circulated as debt via the commercial money circuit. The public sector thus loses its sovereignty, becoming just another borrower.

Until 1694 British royal debts were personal loans to the sovereign. They became the national debt when subject to Parliamentary guarantees as demanded by the commercial investors in the Bank of

England. As was discussed earlier, a major element in the history of modern banking was the need of rulers for loans, mainly to fight wars. This was not a problem for Alexander the Great or the Roman Empire, but as the use of coinage developed the principle of sovereignty became undermined. The control of money shifted from the ruling class to the merchant class.

In the hands of autocratic rulers money creation enabled direct access to labour, provisioning and resources. Though this seigniorage privilege was limited to the ruler and their entourage, money was a medium to secure use value, even if that use was to make war or build extravagant palaces. When prevailing forms of money became privatised by the growing merchant class, as a commodity to be sold as debt or issued as credit, the sovereign power to use money without incurring debt was curtailed. However, the sovereign use of money for direct provisioning, rather than trade, did not pass from rulers to the public. It became captured by the emerging capitalist class. At the same time, the public became responsible for the sovereign debts incurred. From being commanded by autocrats, access to money and provisioning became dependent on debt, labour and commodity exchange. Rather than creating and circulating their own forms of money, rulers became dependent on either taxing private wealth or borrowing.

As Graeber points out, the early years of modern banks saw a shift in state funding. When rulers needed more money and could not raise more tax, they reverted to borrowing, often demanding 'forced' loans. For Graeber, there is a fine line between a ruler demanding taxation and requiring a loan from wealthy citizens when needing additional resources (2011: 338–9). However, there is a critical difference. Taxation implies a sovereign right to command resources, while borrowing creates an obligation to the lender. Although today there would seem to be little difference between rule by an autocratic monarch or by a cartel of bankers, the distinction has an important influence on the modern conception of public debt and the functioning of the two circuits of money.

Large-scale state borrowing reflects a major shift from feudal power to capitalist power. If there is to be a transition to people power the concept of public money needs to be rescued from feudal seigniorage and transferred to the seigniorage of the people. Before sovereigns became reliant on commercial debt, they obtained what they needed by direct appropriation of goods and services or by taxation. To translate this into modern terms, public provisioning through public money would need to reclaim the ability to directly appropriate structures of provisioning through a command over the creation and circulation of money. Before that can be done the concept of national debt needs to be challenged. How did the capitalist class take control of sovereign money and how can it be reclaimed for the people? Debt was the vital element.

When the sovereign began incurring debts rather than raising taxes, it could be seen in two ways. One way would be to see it as an advance taxation. Desan sees tally sticks as fulfilling this function in Britain from at least the thirteenth century (2014: 174). Tallies were receipts for goods and services provided and could be submitted when taxes were due as proof of prepayment. The second way is to see prepayment of money as a loan that will be repaid out of future taxation. In the first case the tally money is created at the point of prepayment and returned to the state at the time of taxation. The second pattern is entirely the opposite. The money is created by the lender, given to the state to spend and then paid back to the private lender out of future taxes. This makes little difference when the lenders are also the major taxpayers. They are merely deferring their own taxes. When the taxpayers and wealth owners are separate groups the distinction between taxation and borrowing becomes critical. Today, the wealthy are the lenders but the whole public is the debtor.

When the Bank of England was set up it lent a range of money forms to the King, often returning to him his own debts. When the Bank took on the role of public currency creator, it was still seen as 'lending' to the public sector. This confused the original role of commercial lenders to the crown with the capacity of the crown to create its own money. What is the status of the money that is being borrowed? Is it a loan based on the private credit of the bankers or is it based on the private creation of public currency? Is the state approaching the central bank as a commercial lender or as the creator of the national currency? This Janus-face confusion continues to this day. Does the national debt involve the public borrowing its own money or is the central bank obtaining a transfer from the 'wealth-creating sector'? The answer is that it is both. The public is borrowing its own money which is then sold as an asset to the financial sector.

Unlike the earlier period when the lender and taxpayer were likely to be the same people, an increasingly powerful capitalist class are directly or indirectly buying sovereign debt while avoiding tax wherever possible. This leaves the rest of the public in the position of paying the rich for the privilege of borrowing their own money. The nation's public currency had been created as a private commodity, lent back to the public and then securitised as national debt. Rather than the right of seigniorage passing to the people, the commercial banks have claimed it, thereby putting the public collectively into the position of debtor via the concept of the national debt. Publicly created money spent by the state was construed as public debt to the banking sector. The public is just another borrower.

Originally, allowing the central banks the role of creating public currency could be seen as a democratic move. The money supply was no longer the prerogative of autocratic power holders or chaotic private banks. However, the ability to create the public currency was not transferred to the public or its representatives, but rather to the commercial banking sector. The structure of the relationship of the central bank to the commercial banks means that the exclusive ability to create money has been lost by the central bank and thus by the public. The result is that the Bank of England guarantees the privately created public currency in circulation (not just bank notes) based on the government's capacity to tax the people. This is the process by which all new money is created as debt, with no formal capacity on the part of the state to access money that is free of the need to repay. As has been argued in Chapter 3, however, the capacity to create public money is implicit in the public money circuit. Public expenditure does not follow taxation and borrowing, it precedes it. A deficit is a surplus of expenditure over mechanisms to reclaim that money. The decision to see this as a debt, rather than the prerogative of the public to create new currency, is a political one.

The politics of public debt is avoided by deeming central banks to be independent, technical institutions. The ability to create money as debt has been passed to the wider banking sector and the central bank is just seen creating notes and electronic money in response to the needs of the banks. This is central to the privatisation of money creation, where the state has moved from being the main creator of public money to being a supplicant 'housewife'. There is no concept of a central bank issuing public money for public benefit in neoliberal handbag economics. Politically this is achieved by limiting the concept of the public to the state and the incumbent government. The superiority of the market is set against the inefficiency and the corruption of power-holders. But this ignores the role of private power-holders. The issue is not that of a choice between public and private power-holders, but concerns the right of the public as a whole to access their own money free of debt in order to provision themselves. Surplus public expenditure need not be 'borrowed' from anyone.

The status of national debt is also confused by its use as a monetary instrument. 'Open market operations' refers to the process by which central banks buy and sell government debt with the aim of influencing interest rates. As previously noted, national debt is also a major source of investment. Far from states being dependent on borrowing from the 'money markets', financial institutions are dependent on the security of sovereign debt. National debt is not a drain on the 'wealth-creating' sectors, it is a source of their wealth. It reflects the continuing process of the private creation of money and the sale of it to the public sector. The sovereign power to create money has been harnessed for the benefit of the capitalist class.

The Misuse of Public Money: Quantitative Easing

Quantitative easing is the creation of new public money. It has been used in a variety of ways, but mainly to buy back sovereign debt or commercial assets/debt. Quantitative easing made transparent the ability of public monetary authorities to create public currency free of debt. The central banks did not have to borrow the money created from any other body. Quantitative easing was first introduced in Japan in 2001 after a decade of deflation. It had little impact, although it may have stopped things getting even worse. In 2013, under Abenomics, Japan announced a new aggressive programme of QE with the aim of doubling the money supply. It remains to be seen if this is successful.

The US launched its quantitative easing policy in December 2008, and peaked at $85 billion per month. It began to be run down in January 2014 and was halted altogether in October of the same year. The programme mainly bought Treasury bonds and mortgage backed securities. The UK implemented a £375 billion QE programme mainly buying government debt. The ECB followed reluctantly in 2015 proposing a 1.1 trillion euro package to be issued at 60 billion euros per month. It was too little, too late, being only around twice the size of the UK's programme and much smaller than the US's $4.5 trillion.

The misuse of public money was twofold. First, the money should have gone to the people not the banks and financial sector. Second, the public debt purchased with the new public money should have been immediately cancelled. This would have reduced the level of public borrowing and undermined the case for austerity. The UK QE programme could have provided around £24,000 to each household but the money was fed entirely into the financial sector. The sole aim was to get the commercial circuit of money working again. In this it largely failed. Most of the money was unspent or went into financial asset growth. Little went into productive industries, which were themselves sitting on mounds of money. Handbag economics was forcing supply side prescriptions (forcing down wages and making labour more 'flexible') with no attention to the collapse in overall demand. People had no money to spend. The lack of money in circulation and widespread tax avoidance also left little public revenue, thereby driving further austerity. While overall inflation was low, even negative, the poor faced high rents and food prices.

Where QE was used to buy commercial assets, it has replaced possibly toxic loans with good public money. Where it has purchased its own sovereign debt it could cancel it, but mostly it has not. There has been huge support given to the financial sector and very little to the public sector, particularly in the UK, where a highly ideological Tory-led government aimed to drive the public sector back to the conditions of the 1930s. The sole focus of QE has been to get investment going again. QE demonstrates the intricacy of the Janus-faces of central banks. In using newly created public money to try to drive up the quantity of money in circulation, central banks are using a sovereign prerogative, the ability to create money *free of debt*, to support the privatisation of money *as debt*. When purchasing sovereign debt with public money, central banks turn only their commercial face to the people by not immediately cancelling that debt. This is because: 'At the highest level – central banks, national treasuries and the major international institutions – policy making is in the hands of highly trained and extremely competent mainstream economists ... with a deep personal and ideological commitment to orthodox macro-economics' (King 2012: 308).

Rather than using QE to rekindle the commercial circuit, public money should be created to sustain a renewed public circuit. For ecological reasons alone, the aim cannot be to return to business as usual. The lesson must be that central banks should never use public money to rescue the private sector. The opportunity must be taken to demonstrate that money must be democratised: 'money is the ultimate technology for the decentralised organisation of society ... only democratic politics provides the sensitivity to current conditions and the legitimacy ... that is necessary for money to work sustainably' (Martin 2014: 272). The role of central banks is critical to the debate about public money. They bring together the sovereign capacity to create the public currency free of debt and the commercial creation of money to sell as debt. The public sector has lost the capacity to do the former and is dependent on the latter. The people as citizens are now debtors to the commercial sector both as taxpayers and private borrowers. Capitalism has captured the right to create money from autocratic monarchs but has used it to fuel its own profit-seeking activities. It must be reclaimed by the people, for the people. The central bank as the banker to banks is using its sovereign prerogative to create money to support the commercial creation of money as debt. It is using its commercial face to sell the public its own money. This must be reversed. The central bank must return the sovereign prerogative of money creation free of debt to the people, for the benefit of the people, as a public resource.

6

Understanding Public Money

This chapter will look at approaches to money that reject the myths identified earlier in this book. In various ways they see money as public and/or social in essence. However, while there is considerable overlap, they are not all in agreement about the nature of money. These approaches, which have already informed much of the preceding discussion, are the state theory of money, the monetary theory of production, modern money theory (MMT) and advocates of monetary reform.

The State Theory of Money

One of the earliest proponents of a public conception of money was the German economist, Georg Knapp (1842–1926). Far from the market-oriented and privatised view of money of contemporary handbag economics, Knapp saw the state as central to the existence of money. In his major work *The State Theory of Money* (1905/1924). Knapp argues that money is not an economic phenomenon linked to the market; it is very much a public phenomenon: 'money is a creature of law' (1924: 1). For this reason he sees the study of the monetary system as a branch of political science and 'the attempt to deduce it without the idea of a State ... [as] ... absurd' (1924: viii). It is states that establish the status of money forms such as coins or public currency notes, or abstract notions such as the pound sterling. Keynes echoed Knapp's view 'that money is peculiarly a creation of the state' (1971: 4), and claims it has been so for four thousand years.

While for conventional economics the first function of money is as a medium of commodity exchange, Knapp sees it as a more general means of payment. Although money is used in market exchange, there are many situations in which payment does not relate to the market, such as fees, fines or taxes. In fact, Knapp sees public administrative payments as a better grounding for the status of money than general acceptance in trade: 'the money of the state is not what is of compulsory general acceptance, but what is accepted at the public pay office' (1924: vii). Knapp acknowledges that commodities of material value (such as precious metal) have been used in exchange, but he does not consider this to be money. In fact, he shares the opinion of this book that money only comes into play when the actual form of payment has no intrinsic value: 'money comes into being when the material is no longer the means of payment' (1924: 25). He goes on to argue that even where money is made of precious materials, 'the soul of the currency is not in the material of the pieces, but in the legal ordinances that regulate their use' (1924: 2). He notes that the first question a trader will ask in a new country is, what is the nature of the currency?

At the time that Knapp was writing, paper money was well established, and he wanted to defend the view that 'the much-derided inconvertible paper money is still money' (1924: 38). Inconvertible here means that it cannot be exchanged for precious metal. Knapp sees all forms of money as a chartal or token ('chartal' derives from the Latin for token). Paper or other non-material money is not inferior to metal money, as both are part of an administrative monetary system: 'Coins are stamped discs made of metal' while 'warrants are stamped discs of paper' (1924: 56).

Knapp's theory offers a very different view of the origin and nature of money from conventional economics, and a very different view of tax. For handbag economics, the state is continually 'stealing the taxpayer's money' instead of leaving it in his or her pocket. Every penny that the state spends is a burden on the taxpayer. The assumption is that money originates outside of the state, as does all value. The state theory of money has a very different view of taxation and the creation of money. Put simply: 'The State ... creates it' (1924: 39). Money is created by the state as a convenience for society. It allows people to pay their debts and dues. Knapp sees it as particularly beneficial to the taxpayer that the state creates the money that it later accepts in payment of tax, as it 'frees us from our debts to the state, for the state, when emitting it, acknowledges that, in receiving, it will accept this means of payment' (1924: 52). What Knapp is describing is the public circuit of money as described in Chapter 3.

Keynes: Facing Both Ways?

Keynes has an ambivalent approach to money. While he adopts a public conception of money in sympathy with Knapp, he also develops a monetary theory of production that puts money in the hands of the market. Keynes appears to start from the perspective of chartalism (money as a token), opening his discussion with the statement that 'today all civilised money ... is chartalist' (1971: 4). He also follows Knapp's view of the role of the state: 'Knapp's chartalism ... the doctrine that money is peculiarly a creation of the state is fully realised' (1971: 4). Unlike the commodity theorists who see money as a medium of exchange emerging out of barter, Keynes is quite clear that money as an accounting mechanism is much more important than the role of money as a medium. A 'money of account' must precede a 'money of payment' as debt and prices must come before the medium of payment (1971: 3).

However, Keynes still retains a key notion of the tangibility of money in the 'thing' that answers to the money of account. This leads to a confusion in his description of 'money proper'. Although 'money proper ... can only exist in relation to a money of account' (1971: 3), it is only 'money proper' that can finally discharge a debt. For Keynes state money is 'money proper' (1971: 5). As has already been discussed, this raises questions about the status of bank-created money which exists only as an account: can it be money proper? To confuse the issue further, Keynes' definition of state money seems to include non-state forms: 'I propose to include as State money not only money which is itself compulsory legal tender but also money which the State or the central bank undertakes to accept in payments to itself or to exchange for compulsory legal-tender money' (1971: 6). Keynes identifies two main forms of money: commodity and representative. The latter can be 'fiat', having no convertible base or 'objective standard', or 'managed' where it is related to some 'objective standard'. The use of terms such as 'representative' and 'objective standard' indicates that

Keynes thought there was, or should be, some concrete base to money where 'commodity money and managed money are ... related to an objective standard of value' (1971: 7). Keynes sees managed money as a hybrid between a commodity money and fiat money. In modern economies it is 'the most generalised form of money' (1971: 7). He sees the British Bank Act of 1844 as cementing the role of managed, representative money. In seeing representative money as a modern phenomenon, Keynes has to 'leave aside' older paper forms such as were used in ancient China, or the failed John Law experiment in early eighteenth-century France (1971: 13).

For Keynes, the state's role is to enable full employment and shared prosperity. The public use of money is to create sufficient demand for the private sector to operate at full capacity when private momentum fails. What, then, is the basis of that private momentum? What is the role of money in the productive circuit? Is there an alternative 'endogenous' source of new money that emerges from within the commercial sector, that is, the commercial money circuit as described earlier?

The Monetary Theory of Production: Money Circuit Theory

Keynes' view of the importance of money in capitalist production was taken up by the Italian economist Augusto Graziani (1933–2014), who was also influenced by Marx and Schumpeter (Bellofiore 2013). Graziani explored bank finance as central to capital formation in his money circuit theory. This sees money as both the key to production and the goal of production for capitalism. Money is borrowed or created to pay for the cost of production; this is then repaid following the process of exchange and consumption, and the circle turns again.

Money circuit theory's 'endogenous' view of money rejects the idea that the state can impose any top down 'exogenous' control of the money supply. Nor can exogenous financial discipline be imposed by a 'natural' money such as gold. In particular, it rejects the idea that state manipulation of central bank reserves can have an impact on bank lending. According to Rossi, there should be no need to have 'vertical', i.e. central bank, management of the money system, as any issue of new credit would always be accompanied by new production and consumption. Rather optimistically, writing before the crash,

Rossi dismisses the possibility of financialisation eclipsing production. Without production, 'financial markets would be meaningless' (Rossi 2007: 34). This view of the emergence of (capitalist) money in commercial trade has more in common with conventional economic theory than with the state money theorists. Against the state theory of money, Rossi stresses the importance of bank-created money: 'Contrary to what the advocates of chartalism claim, taxation powers, fiscal policy and government are not necessary conditions to account for, and to explain, the origins, nature and value of money' (2007: 20). For Rossi, money is 'a creature' of banks, rather than the state (2007: 21).

Money is created by banks when producers borrow money in order to launch the circuit of production: 'Money's value is based ... on production and banking systems working together to associate a real object (that is, produced output) to a numerical counter (money)' (Rossi 2007: 20). While placing the banking system at the centre of its analysis of money's origin, money circuit theory rejects the fractional reserve story of bank lending, starting from deposits of precious metal. Instead, it supports the view taken in this book that bank lending grew out of personal loans and promises of payment. Banks acted as a 'third partner' in commodity exchange. Based on their own creditworthiness, bankers agreed to 'cash' a debtor's promise to a creditor for a fee and/or a discount (paying less than the face value), pending later payment to the bank by the debtor. This meant the creditor had ready money from a creditworthy source in place of a personal debt, while the banker took the risk of non-payment.

Unlike conventional theory, money circuit theory does not see money as a neutral reflection of the circuit of production. Money is not a creature of law, but of capitalism: an active force determined by conflict and structural power. It harnesses both household borrowing and state deficits to fuel capitalist production and accumulation. As this book argues, under neoliberal handbag economics the money supply is in the hands of the banks and emerges as debt. Without that debt (confusingly described as credit), capitalism cannot accumulate (Mellor 2010a). Debt makes possible 'both market exchange and the more extensive set of relationships known as capitalism' (Smithin 2009: 59). For full 'elasticity of credit' to be available, it is necessary that bank money creation has no artificial limits such as the need to match loans to deposits. If debt creation ceases it is disastrous for capitalist economies, as the credit crunch that finally triggered the 2007–8 financial crisis showed. While money circuit theory provides an important analysis of the commercial circuit of money, and reveals the importance of the private creation of money to the survival of capitalism, it does not address the possibility of a public circuit of money. The two views of money have been brought together in modern money theory (MMT).

Modern Money Theory (MMT)

Modern money theory has been developed by a group of heterodox economists, many of whom are linked to the University of Missouri-Kansas City in the US. MMT's analysis combines Knapp's state theory of money, Mitchell Innes's chartalist views of money as a token, Keynes' monetary theory of production and proposals for government economic intervention, and Abba Lerner's (1943) advocacy of 'functional finance' that explicitly called for the state to take an active financial role in supporting real economic performance by 'printing money' where necessary. The overall aim of MMT is to achieve the Keynesian ideal of a fully operating economy: 'Functional finance ... says that sovereign government ought to operate fiscal and monetary policy to achieve full employment' (Wray 2012: 258).

The primary aim of modern money theorists such as Wray is that economic theory and practice should be based on an understanding of the way modern money systems *actually* work, rather than the false assumptions of conventional thinking. MMT sees contemporary money systems as based on fiat, largely endogenous, bank-created money, but also with a strong role for the state, particularly the central bank. It challenges many of the myths of handbag economics, particularly its aim of minimising the state (Wray 2009) and 'deficit hysteria' (Nersisyan and Wray 2010). Spending more money than raised in taxes is an important monetary and fiscal instrument for MMT, particularly when needed to boost the economy.

While MMT shares with the endogenous money theorists the view that central banks cannot control the privatised money supply, its main focus is on the monetary role of the state, in what this book describes as the public circuit of money. Like the state theory of money, MMT sees states as nominating a public currency and establishing its authority through demanding it back as taxation. People need to acquire that currency if they are to pay their obligations as citizens. At the same time, public authorities must be willing to accept that currency as fulfilment of those obligations: 'The currency is issued by a sovereign government when it spends and received by government in payment of taxes and other payments to the government' (Wray 2012: 264). MMT argues that the links between the monetary and fiscal (tax and spend) circuit have been misunderstood. Far from taxes being raised to pay for public expenditure the public money circuit is entirely the other way around. Governments create money through public expenditure that is credited to private/business bank accounts. This increases the overall money in circulation. When the government imposes taxes it withdraws money by taking money from bank accounts. Tax can be used as both a monetary and a fiscal instrument. It can regulate the money supply as well as influence actual expenditure. However, there is no direct link between state expenditure and taxation. There is no fund that the state draws upon. Public spending and taxation are two separate mechanisms linked by accounting systems.

MMT rejects the conventional view of money as being primarily a medium of exchange. Instead money is seen mainly as an accounting mechanism, both as a unit of account and a record of account. MMT distinguishes between money as a unit of account (which need not necessarily exist in any tangible form) and the money things that represent those values, e.g. the pound coin or the keystrokes that add money to bank accounts. Money is seen as endogenous because it rises up through a structure of debts and payments. All money is an IOU: 'money is always a debt' (Wray 2012: 264). MMT argues that money can never settle a debt because by definition it has no value, it is not a commodity, it is a promise: 'money things are liabilities, obligations, IOU's of their issuer' (Wray 2012: 262). When someone makes a payment they are issuing a promise to the recipient. However, private citizens making such a payment cannot guarantee the value of that promise themselves. They therefore pay with public currency cash, which has automatic status, or pay through a bank which has a more credible form of money. In turn, the bank has limits to its credibility so it exchanges its monetary promises into state money. That is, money represents a hierarchy of IOUs with the state at the top.

MMT maintains the distinction between bank money and state money as high powered money (HPM). HPM is coins, paper dollars, bank reserves and government bills and bonds (Wray 2012: 162). High powered money is the apex of the series of IOU promises represented by money things: 'liabilities of households and firms are converted to demand deposits of banks ... and bank IOUs are convertible to government currency ... HPM' (Wray 2012: 262). Given the hierarchy of debt, it is ultimately the state on which the whole tottering system rests (Wray 2004: 260). However, this is not because the state has a different form of money (for example reserves of gold) but because it has a superior form of credit. Its promise to pay has the backing of its capability to both tax and create new money.

What is important for MMT is the sovereign power to nominate the monetary unit and the capacity to create the money things: 'When a government spends, it does so by creating "high powered money", HPM, that is, by crediting bank reserves. When it taxes it destroys HPM, debiting bank reserves' (Wray 2012: 197). However, it cannot exercise that power if it does not have monetary sovereignty. MMT argues that states must not be tied to formal exchange rate structures, such as the gold standard, or be tied into any other currency, as this would reduce their internal monetary autonomy. For this reason MMT favours floating exchange rates. A major problem with this stipulation is that floating exchange rates have been one of the major sources of instability in the financial and monetary system, with the expansion of derivative speculation and loss of public control of money systems.

Like this book, MMT argues that a monetarily sovereign state is not like a household that has to 'live within its means'. A sovereign state can never run out of its own currency. This would not be true for a local or regional state, but a sovereign state that is responsible for issuing its own money supply, and able to float its currency against others, cannot be insolvent within its own monetary boundaries. A sovereign state can always create the money it needs to maintain full productive capacity. MMT follows Keynes in seeing state employment as the best mechanism to support the economy. States should not just be lenders of last resort, but employers of last resort.

MMT provides a fundamental critique of conventional monetary thinking and adopts the Keynesian position that the economy should work for the benefit of the people. Wray argues that the ability of entrepreneurs to use borrowed money to harness existing assets implies a social obligation to give something at least equivalent back to the society: 'we can view all commodity production as social' (Wray 2012: 271). MMT's strength lies in its analysis of the existing monetary framework. It is not arguing about what *ought* to be, but about what the real dynamics *are*. It has a clear role for public money and demonstrates that there is no monetary justification for austerity. However, modern money theorists do not propose denying banks the right to create endogenous money; they just want to bring the banks and market within the framework of public purpose. MMT appears to see the public and commercial circuits as continuing to run alongside each other. This is a very different position from advocates of monetary reform who want to see the end of the capacity of banks to create the public currency as debt.

Monetary Reform

The main concern of monetary reform centres on the power of banks to create the public currency as debt. However, monetary reform is a broad church and runs from Austrians who want to completely privatise the money supply, to advocates of various forms of public money. All want to constrain or eliminate money supply created through debt. Austrians want to control credit creation and create 'sound money' by imposing a 100 per cent reserve (possibly re-establishing a gold standard or equivalent). This would limit lending to the amount of reserves available. The market would then decide on the allocation of the limited supply of money. Advocates of public money want all initial money supply to be filtered through the public sector and thereby gain seigniorage, the ability of money creators to extract economic benefit from money creation.

Unlike the money circuit theorists who see banks as performing an intermediary function in trading systems, monetary reformers (particularly from the market group) tend to recount the 'goldsmiths story' (there are several versions of this on the web). As described earlier, the story recounts how people left their gold for safe-keeping with goldsmiths who then issued paper to represent the gold. When the goldsmiths found that people didn't come back for the actual gold they lent paper against the gold over and over again, in increasing volume, making more profit each time. This is seen as leading to the widespread development of fractional reserve banking in modern banking systems. The fractional reserve notion implies that there are two types of money, the 'real' money that is a deposit/reserve that is backed in some way, and bank-issued money as debt, which is not. Banks are seen as creating a vast mountain of 'credit money' on a very small reserve of 'real' money. They are 'lending money they haven't got'. Rather than seeing banking as a service to capitalism as the money circuit theorists do, it is represented as a fraud against the depositors, even, in some more extreme approaches, as a conspiracy of greedy and dishonest bankers.

The Case for the Market

A leading advocate of the market approach to monetary reform is the Spanish Professor of Political Economy, Jesus Huerta de Soto. He sees the origin of boom and bust cycles as lying in 'artificial credit expansions' in the banking system as against 'the prior or genuine savings of citizens'. He sees the banks as issuing 'huge doses of fiduciary media' based on the limited 'gold originally deposited in their vaults' (2010: 2). This distorts the 'real productive structure' of the 'spontaneous ... unhampered free market' which otherwise would 'correctly invest all funds previously saved by economic agents' (2010: 5). 'Prior, genuine, real savings' should be the only basis for investment as this restricts consumption of existing production to leave space for new 'spontaneous' businesses to emerge (2010: 8). De Soto puts the blame for the financial crisis squarely on the credit bubble 'orchestrated and directed by Central Banks', pointing out that in recent years money supply has been growing at an average rate of 10 per cent a year (2010: 15). As there was no concurrent increase in the price of consumer goods and services, this level of money expansion was largely ignored. Personal debt and collapsed savings avoided the 'necessary sacrifice and discipline ... of voluntary saving' (2010: 16). He critiques the 'mark to market' accounting systems (pricing all assets at current market value) that pro-cyclically drive both booms and busts (2010: 20), but is adamant that the 'spontaneous order of the unhampered market is not responsible' (2010: 21).

De Soto agrees with the state/public approach to monetary reform that the administration of national currency supply has been handed as a 'legal privilege given by the state to private bankers' (2010: 22). This he applauds, seeing public money as a form of 'real socialism' that has nationalised what he sees as previously private money (2010: 21–2). Central banks have been created 'precisely to bail out banks' and create liquidity at points of crisis (2010: 4). His solution is to return total control of money to the private sector by freezing the money supply at its current level, shrinking the state, 'freeing' the labour market and thus (he assumes) liberating money for 'real' investment. Bank deposits would become mere storage for previously existing money, and banks would return to being intermediaries between savers and borrowers (something with which other monetary reformers would agree).

The question then becomes whether there should be any source of future money supply and on what basis. De Soto's prescription is predictable: 'full privatization of the current, monopolistic, and fiduciary state-issued paper base money, and its replacement with a classic pure gold standard' (2010: 30). As a transition he advocates the printing of new bank notes to match all current deposit accounts, which would be handed to the banks to 'back' those deposits. In return, all the existing assets of the banks would be used to 'liberate' (i.e. pay off) Treasury bonds. Presumably the fixed stock of money would then circulate in perpetuity. This 100 per cent reserve approach contrasts with more socially oriented reformers who advocate the pro-active creation of new fiat public money. As Cook (2007) points out, within the monetary reform movement there is a 'raging controversy' over whether to advocate a return to some equivalent to the gold standard.

The Case for Public Money

Over time, whoever controls the money system controls the society.

Stephen Zarlenga, Director, American Monetary Institute

The more socially oriented group of monetary reformers agree that the challenge is to the role of debt in bank money creation. This is contrasted with the state's capacity to create money free of debt. A main concern is that state-created money (as notes and coin) has shrunk to around 3 per cent of money issued in a country like Britain, leaving bank-created money as the only effective source of new currency. Radical monetary reformers seek to overturn what they see as the shift from public money to bank debt. To reverse this trend, the ability to create money must be removed from the banking sector and returned to the public or social sectors (Robertson 2012, Douthwaite 1999, Huber and Robertson 2000, Robertson and Bunzl 2003). The benefit of the capacity to create the public currency once claimed by rulers would then be passed to the people. The public could reclaim the benefit of first use of the money for public, social or environmental purposes, that is, exercise 'seigniorage'.

Many of the campaigners for monetary reform combine environmental and social justice concerns. The green concern is that when most money is created as bank debt, growth becomes endemic to the system. More money must constantly be borrowed to make repayments with interest, entailing destructive pressure for continuing growth and expansion in the economy (Douthwaite 2000: 30, Cato 2009: 38). Ecofeminists are also concerned that a gendered, debt-driven economy can never be the basis of a sustainable provisioning economy (Hutchinson, Mellor and Olsen 2002, Mellor 2010a, 2010b). Similar sentiments are expressed by those who link new forms of money to a commitment to local production and exchange (Seyfang 2011).

The American Monetary Institute (AMI) is campaigning for the power to issue all public currency to be returned to the people. Through a supportive Congressman, Dennis Kucinich, it proposed a NEED Act (National Emergency Employment Defense Act), which aimed to end the power of private banks to create public currency as debt and restore that power to Congress. It could then create and spend debt-free money to maintain a stable economy without inflation or deflation. Private banks would retain the role of acting as monetary intermediaries, using their own money or money deposited with them by investors. Rather than austerity and debt, AMI claims that the NEED Act would bring an immediate end to the growth of the national debt; fund investment in infrastructure to create millions of jobs; provide a tax-free grant to all citizens to stimulate the economy; and begin paying off the national debt as it comes due, to reduce the interest burden on taxpayers.

James Robertson in the UK has long argued that the public money supply should be created and used in the public interest. He wants all new money to be created by a public agency and spent into circulation for public benefit, including a citizen income that would be 'predis-tributive' (2012: 128). Jackson and Dyson argue that 'no industry in the world ... conforms less to the principles of capitalism than banking', given the high levels of public financial support it has received (2012: 280). They want to assign the money creation task to an independent monetary authority that would respond only to inflationary or deflationary triggers: 'money would be created as long as inflation is low, steady and within the target range' (2012: 310). Like Robertson, they want any new money created to serve public purposes, such as public expenditure, citizen income and support for the 'real economy'. In this way, the 'privilege and benefits' of money creation would be returned to the people' (2012: 281).

A problem for monetary reform is how the decision to create new public money would be made. Jackson and Dyson, as just noted, propose an independent monetary authority, a Money Creation Committee. This would make decisions on technical grounds, mainly related to the level of inflation and/or credit need within the 'real', i.e. non-financial, economy (2012: 214). While this would undermine the financial sector, it would support non-finance capitalism. Effectively the private sector would still drive the money supply. Tying the money supply to the current 'real economy' would also limit the ability to expand public currency into new areas such as a citizen income or payment for currently unpaid labour. Jackson and Dyson do, however, allow that the remit of the Money Creation Committee could be amended to reflect democratically determined priorities. The proposal in this book is that public demand for public provisioning would drive the money supply. Most of this money would be spent within a social or public provisioning system. This money could then 'trickle out' to the commercial sector with overall supply regulated by taxation.

Public Money: IOU or Seigniorage?

There is a basic disagreement between MMT and monetary reform about the nature of public money. Josef Huber, a leading monetary reformer, has challenged MMT's view of states as heading a hierarchy of IOUs. This would imply that the creation of public money in some way creates a liability on the part of the state. In creating money, Huber claims, the state does not owe anybody anything. Knapp seems to be on his side, saying that in nominating the public currency, the state is not creating a liability. In general usage, token (chartal) money does not imply a future debt, 'it is a true payment' (Knapp 1924: 51). It is not 'a provisional satisfaction still leaving something to be done on the part of the state' (1924: 50). Knapp is adamant that paper money is 'not an acknowledgement of the state's indebtedness' (1924: 50). It is the prerogative of the state to decide what form the currency will take and then to create it. States created the coin and now they create the paper money (i.e. bank notes). Both are equally valid and neither are a claim on the state. For Knapp money is an administrative convenience, issued to enable economic activities to take place.

What is the difference, then, between Huber's view of the sovereign state's debt-free currency and MMT's sovereign high powered money as an IOU? Huber describes his approach as New Currency Theory (NCT) while claiming that MMT reflects a 'banking school' view. The currency and banking schools were on opposite sides of a debate in the first half of the nineteenth century. The banking school stressed the importance of bank lending in enabling the economy to develop, and opposed the idea of any artificial limits on the ability of money to grow in response to demand. The currency school was concerned that uncontrolled lending by banks would spin the money supply out of control. The currency school won the battle but lost the war. In 1844 the British Banking Act gave a monopoly to the Bank of England in the production of bank notes but capped the number that could be issued. What the Act did not anticipate was the expansion of purely accounting activities within banks and between banks. It did not recognise that banks had the ability to create new currency as bank loans administered through bank accounts.

Huber supports the 'currency school' which argues that money does not need to be loaned into circulation, but can be spent into circulation free of debt, interest and redemption (2014: 41). It is then able to circulate as a symbol of the exchange of use values. He sees MMT as arguing that money can only be borrowed into existence. Jackson and Dyson agree: 'Instead of treating money as a liability of the issuer (as is the current set up for bank notes), we treat money as a token, issued by the state. This money is accepted and used by people and businesses because they are confident they can exchange these tokens with other people for goods or services of equivalent value' (2012: 311). The only asset backing public currency is 'the productive capacity of the economy'; money should be seen not as a debt but as 'equity in the commonwealth' (Jackson and Dyson 2012: 319). Blain agrees: 'In restricting the meaning of money to debt, MMT perpetuates the interest-bearing debt money system'; instead 'a nation's money should be understood like shares of a corporation' (Blain 2014: 82–3).

However, the MMT concept of a sovereign IOU only seems to mean that creators of money must accept their own money back again: 'The nature of the obligation of the issuer is this: one must always accept one's IOU in payment to oneself' (Wray 2012: 262). This is the essence of the public money circuit as described in this book. Public money creation or expenditure starts the circuit which is only completed when the equivalent money is returned. Until then, the money is free to circulate. It is only the creators of money that can finally cancel the circuit. Currency circulates in both the commercial and public circuits until the original debt is returned to the lender, or the public money is returned in taxation or other payments.

For Huber, the public monetary prerogative has three aspects: determining the national unit of account (currency prerogative); issuing the money denominated in that currency (legal tender prerogative); and benefiting from the first-user advantage of new money (prerogative of seigniorage) (2014: 50). MMT would be in agreement with the first two prerogatives, but rejects the concept of seigniorage as it implies there is no obligation on the part of the issuer of money. Seigniorage also implies a source of monetary power that is not endogenously driven by grassroots demand. Huber agrees with MMT that public money is just a token, but contends that it has sovereign power.

Like most monetary reformers, Huber sees seigniorage as deriving from the historical sovereign power to create and spend money. Rulers traditionally had that benefit when issuing public currency, but this has been usurped by the banks. Seigniorage implies that the creator of new money is not in the position of a debtor (issuing an IOU), but they are a beneficiary of the nominal value of the money: they are getting 'something for nothing'. From an MMT perspective, Wray agrees that 'all sovereign governments can be said to get something for nothing, since they purchase by keystrokes'. However he goes on to argue: 'but that is not seigniorage: it results from the fact that sovereign government imposes liabilities on its population: taxes, fees and fines' (2012: 138). The power comes from the sovereign power to impose taxes, not the efficacy of the money itself.

Whereas MMT sees government IOUs as sovereign money creation and an asset to the wider financial sector, Huber argues that government debt, is just that, debt: 'MMT's re-interpretation of the issue of government IOUs as an issue of sovereign money, thus depicting government as a creditor rather than a debtor, is misguided' (Huber 2014: 47). Rather than creating independent sovereign money, the state has succumbed to what has been identified in this book as the commercial circuit. Borrowing is not the creation of high powered public money, rather governments have ended up using bank-created money by default. Sovereign debt is not sovereign money and central banks only have a commercial face: 'central banks today act much more often as bank of the banks than bank of the state' ... 'the banking industry fully determines the entire process of money creation, whereas the government, far from being monetarily sovereign, is indebted to and dependent on the banks' ... 'unless a state decides to recapture from the banking industry the full and unimpaired monetary prerogative of a sovereign state ... the government of that state is not really sovereign and will have to give in to the demands of the banking industry' (Huber 2014: 48–9).

Ganssmann also sees both the government and the central bank as having been overtaken by the dominance of bank-created money: 'there is no question that modern central bank money is credit money and that the modern financial system has made it increasingly difficult to distinguish money from credit instruments' (2011: 134). By credit money in this context he means money created through debt. Ganssmann also challenges the pairing of credit with debt in MMT which sees money as being at the same time a credit (to the holder) and a debt (to the issuer). Ganssmann draws a distinction between a debt which is a promise to pay in the future and a credit, that is the belief that the form of money held will be accepted in the future. Not all transfers of money imply a debt: 'paying with a coin or a central bank note implies an immediate transfer of purchasing power to the amount stated on the money object, with no further strings attached' (2011: 133).

Modern money theorists are much less concerned about government borrowing than monetary reformers. They see it as a technical exercise that injects and extracts money from circulation. Because they see no necessary limit to the creation of sovereign money, old debts can always be paid by new money. There is no drain on the national currency, 'government spends by "creating money" through keystroke entries to balance sheets' (Wray 2012: 197). The task that MMT sets itself is to get the benign role of government monetary activity, particularly deficits, accepted in the mainstream by explaining 'how money "works" in the modern economy' (Wray 2012: ix). Wray sees the sovereign capacity to create money as a major source of wealth and stability if used correctly (2012: 277).

It seems that monetary reform and MMT are at cross purposes. Public money is both debt free and a promise of future acceptance. It is debt free in that it is free from the commercial need to create money as debt. As argued in this book, the decision to deny the public the right to create money free of debt is entirely ideological. However the money created would still embody a promise. Those who initially receive it in payment or allocation will expect to be able to exchange it for goods and services. People within a money system must continue to accept it in payment. There is 'an underlying *collective* commitment of money users' and a public authority to support it (Ganssmann

2011: 127, emphasis in the original). In this the concept of seigniorage is helpful.

In this book seigniorage has been used to refer to the benefit of first use of money over and above the cost of its production. For most types of money there is very little cost: setting up a bank loan, notching a tally stick, printing a note. For people who cannot create money there is no seigniorage; they must earn the money or borrow it from someone else. Seigniorage therefore implies a lack of reciprocation. When traditional rulers offered public currency as payment they were merely acknowledging in money terms their autocratic claim to harness resources. Unlike the rest of their population, they did not have to give up goods and resources for that money. However, if rulers lose control of their money supply, their seigniorage will cease. Today, banks exercise seigniorage as they do not have to do anything to 'earn' the money they create by a keyboard stroke. As lenders of newly created money, the only obligation they have is to accept the same form of currency back in payment of the debt. Any profit over and above the cost of administering the debt, and allowing for default, accrues to the bank.

Reclaiming public seigniorage in money creation is essential if democracy is to replace debt as the foundation of the public currency. That would require reclaiming control of the supply of public currency: the public circuit of money would become the primary circuit. Benefit from first use of public money within the circuit would then accrue to the people. It would be used for the provision of democratically determined goods and services. The democratic public money circuit is a promise of the people to the people, something they owe to themselves. The money is both an entitlement and an obligation. This would seem to mirror the MMT concept of money as representing credit-debt relations. What the concept of seigniorage provides is a recognition of the benefit of the power to create money. It also provides a language with which to assert the right of the people to inherit what was once the ruler's prerogative; to use money to command labour and resources, not for profit, but for the benefit of the people. However, they are also the producers of those benefits. Public money therefore enables people to claim services for themselves, from themselves.

From its endogenous perspective, MMT sees money as emerging from a hierarchy of IOUs over which states can have little control. MMT 'shares ... the view that the central bank cannot control the money supply or bank reserves' (Wray 2012: 97). This is the very thing that monetary reformers want to challenge. They take an 'exogenous' approach where the money supply needs to be determined outside of the commercial money circuit. It is hard to see how an endogenous money could escape from market forces. From the perspective of sufficiency provisioning, it is the debt-based money system that is exogenous, forcing commercial values in place of use values. However, a democratised public money circuit could be endogenous, that is, seen as bottom up rather than top down. The democratic convergent and cascading model of decision-making as described in Chapter 3 would be endogenous in this sense. It would provide a way of extending debt-free money to members of society such as those doing unpaid domestic labour. Despite its rejection of monetary reform, MMT is very helpful in defending the viability of public money creation. But its overall theory leaves the public money circuit as merely a support mechanism to the commercial circuit.

An historical view of money shows that the monetary reformers and MMT are both right. What they are identifying are different aspects of contemporary money systems coming from distinct historical roots. As discussed in Chapter 4, money has both a sovereign heritage and a private, commercial heritage. Modern banking has combined these two. Banks create money endogenously by issuing debt, but it is not bank money, it is national currency. As such it is a liability on the people.

Theorising Public Money

This book has put forward the view that there are two monetary circuits in contemporary economies, a public money circuit and a commercial money circuit. Both create and circulate the public currency. The difference between them is that one is based on debt, the other is not. The case has been made that the commercial circuit relies upon the capacity of the public money circuit to create the public currency free of debt. What do the theories of money discussed above contribute to this analysis?

The state theory of money supports the central role of public authority in the establishment of a public currency. It confirms the view that money is a social and public phenomenon, not a product of commodity exchange. 'Making the money that forms the public currency is a governance project ... a constitutional undertaking' (Desan 2014: 1).

Monetary circuit theory has provided analysis of the commercial money circuit and the power of endogenous money creation. Bank-created debt drives this circuit. Money circuit's analysis of how banks work as 'third party' intermediaries between creditors and debtors challenges the commodity money depositor/fractional reserve multiplier myth. The circuit does not start from some externally generated 'real money', the loan itself generates the deposit. If there is no 'real money', what do those deposits represent? In the era of private money it was the overall wealth of the bank or banker and the confidence that the circuit of money would keep flowing. The complication comes when a private credit note is designated as public currency. This is the dilemma that this book explores, when privately created money becomes a public responsibility. Endogenous theories of money see public monetary authorities as reactive and unable to control bank lending. This view has been validated by the crisis.

MMT and monetary reform can be challenged as being not necessarily critical of the market or anti-capitalist. In fact, MMT can be seen as a prescription for making the market more effective with public support. Also its demand that currencies float if monetary sovereignty is to be achieved is problematic given the level of speculation and global flows of hot money involved. The radicalism of monetary reform depends on whether it is seen as an end in itself, or as part of a wider radical programme to challenge capitalism and conventional growth-driven economics. The question of democratic control of the money supply is also important. Jackson and Dyson (2012) propose a national monetary budget set by an independent monetary authority. The proposal in this book is to determine the money supply through convergent and cascading budgets. Independent assessment of the monetary implications would be secondary. As explained in Chapter

3, a democratically determined money supply cannot be based on the status quo, or be established before aggregate needs are expressed. How much money is to be created will depend on the demands of sufficiency provisioning. That is a matter for the democratic process to ascertain. A democratised money supply would be both a benefit and a liability. It would be a benefit for the people to be 'paid' by the people collectively provisioning themselves.

The question remains whether action around money at the public level, as MMT or monetary reformers recommend, will be sufficient to challenge capitalism. I would argue that it is important but not sufficient. What monetary reform would do is remove a major source of power for capitalism, the ability to create money. It also provides a powerful mechanism in public hands to enable sufficiency provisioning. However, capitalist and neoliberal structures of power and ownership will also need to be confronted. In doing so, action around money is an underappreciated additional aspect of that challenge.

7

Public Money: Beyond the Borders

This book has argued that a public currency does not emerge from the market, it relies on social trust and public authority. It therefore needs to be located within a social and public framework. Creation and circulation of the public currency cannot be based on debt, as this leads to crisis. The public money supply needs at its centre the creation of public money, that is, public currency created and circulated free of debt. Both publicly and privately created money is fiat money; there is no 'backing' for it except the provisioning capacity of those who live within that monetary community.

To say that money is public and social is not to be atavistic. It doesn't rely on some long-standing cultural identity. Currency is exchanged between complete strangers from a variety of cultural backgrounds. Monetary systems can be much wider than national borders. Several currencies have achieved the status of 'world money'. This implies global social trust and public authority for that money, even where the authority rests in a particular national economy. However, the dominance of privatised control of public currencies has meant that currency relations between countries have been driven by commercial considerations and the social and public nature of money is obscured. The opportunity to build global social and public monetary relations is rejected in favour of a competitive global market that exploits relative currency values.

Up to this point, the discussion of public money has assumed a sovereign public able to democratically control their supply of public currency. This becomes highly problematic when currencies interact with each other, particularly in an unregulated global market. As Eichengreen points out, the globalisation of capitalism drove financial deregulation: 'it became impossible to keep domestic markets tightly regulated once international transactions were liberalised' (2008: 229). Finance and banking systems spread across the globe, becoming increasingly entangled. Having gone beyond the control of their countries of origin, they began to impact on public policy in other countries. For example, US financial interests are reported to have put huge pressure on Greece and Ireland not to default, or let their banks fail, because of the high level of US holding of 'swaps', that is, insurances against just those eventualities. Unlike Iceland which saw a clean break by letting their banks fail, Greece, but most particularly Ireland, broke the people, not the banks.

From 1971 control over national currencies was undermined by the movement towards floating exchange rates. Individual countries faced a choice between floating their own currencies or joining a currency union as in the Eurozone (Eichengreen 2008: 228). Floating exchange rates are effectively a condition of global barter as currencies rise and fall against each other. Money has been defined in this book as the representation of a common nominal value under which relative entitlements and obligations can be expressed. When currencies face each other, they effectively become commodities haggling over their relative 'price'. This creates vast potential for financial speculation. The globalisation of production has been swamped by the global trade in financial derivatives. At the peak of the boom, derivative trading was ten times global GDP, with most transactions having no direct relationship to traded goods. By the end of the twentieth century, currency trading was 95 per cent speculative as against 5 per cent for actual goods and services (Rowbotham 2000: 181). Even then, much of the movement of goods was within transnational companies. Currency trading continues to be big business, estimated at over $5 trillion per day.

The privatisation of the money supply at both national and global level created a huge surplus of money that led to global flows of hot money to parts of the world where it could best exploit cheap labour, weak currencies and minimal social, economic and environmental protection. This destabilised local economies and saw dramatic increases in debt, as developing countries borrowed extensively in stronger currencies in order to enable development and participation in global trade. The 'carry trade' saw money borrowed in countries with lower interest rates and invested where rates were higher, ready to move on again at any time. Hedging against currency movements became a major function of the financial sector and fuelled the huge growth of derivatives. As time progressed, it also became clear that there was dubious speculative activity in foreign exchange trading that acted against the interest of clients, an activity that is now under investigation. Exchange traders were buying ahead of their client's request for foreign exchange thus pushing up the rate the client could be charged.

As Greens have long argued, global trade for purely financial gain becomes uneconomic if the ecological damage including air, land or sea miles travelled is factored in. For this reason, Greens urge production and consumption to be as close to home as possible. Any cross-border trade should minimise environmental damage and pay the producer a fair price. While globalisation has created huge global disparities in wealth and widespread conflict, new technologies have brought the world closer together. Satellite and mobile phone communication have linked people, and the movement of money, across the globe.

The aim of sufficiency provisioning must be to capture the benefits of global communication and interaction without exploiting people or planet. For this, the calculation cannot be monetary. Money must be a means of international solidarity, not the driver of global speculation and exploitative trade. Money at the global level should enable socially just and ecologically sustainable provisioning, just as at the local or national level. The social and public nature of money should be used as the basis for the global exchange of use value not exchange purely for monetary profit. What then are the possibilities of democratically controlled public money at the global level? This chapter will explore how global money systems have operated and then look at alternative proposals.

The Gold Standard: Money as Myth

The aim of tying public currencies to gold reflects one of the most persistent myths about money: that it should embody, or be tied to, something of intrinsic value. The amount of money in circulation then becomes driven by that 'exogenous' value, not the needs of the people who use that money. As explained earlier, the myth of gold sees the origin of money in precious metal coinage, ignoring the many other forms of money in human societies. Even then, the social and public nature of coinage is not recognised.

The earliest coinage was mainly silver or silver-alloy. In the middle ages rulers tried hard to keep coinage circulating with limited amounts of metal: the silver penny in Britain (Desan 2014: 9) or the 'bracteates' of the Holy Roman Empire. The latter were 'a totally wretched and ugly little disc of metal, very thin, of low fineness' which because of their uncertain value circulated very quickly and led to relative prosperity (Douthwaite 1999: 46–7). During this period there was a great deal of construction work, particularly of churches and cathedrals, and wages and earnings were sufficient for a comfortable lifestyle. Douthwaite argues that this 'golden age' was ended by gold. While local populations were happy to honour the ugly little discs, they were not suitable for international trade. That is, beyond the border the money system did not work. To deal with this problem, the Italian trading cities instituted commodity money, where the intrinsic value aimed to reflect nominal value. As the use of gold coinage spread, domestic economies slowed down, rather than speeded up. Gold coins were often in short supply as many 'disappeared into socks and mattresses' (Douthwaite 1999: 47). Wages and employment fell, and rulers found it difficult to extract taxes and had to resort to borrowing. Even at such an early stage, it appeared that what is good for international trade is not necessarily good for economies within individual countries.

In Britain, the attempt to link the new forms of money, particularly paper, to a fixed standard was implemented in the early eighteenth century. Any paper money used in payment could be exchanged for gold to the equivalent value on demand. Under the standard, nations were supposed to limit the issue of paper money to the amount of gold they held. However, whenever more money was needed, usually because of war, the gold standard was suspended. Although the notional link with gold was maintained for nearly 400 years, its high point as the basis for interaction between currencies operated most effectively from the second half of the nineteenth century to the First World War.

The role of gold in international trading has had a mixed response, some seeing it as heralding a golden age of global trade through stabilising currencies, others as having a highly negative impact leading to worldwide depression. For Mark Blyth, the gold standard was 'a major contributory cause of the two worst economic recessions in world history: the 1870s and the 1930s' (2013: 180). In the latter case, Churchill's decision to put Britain back on the gold standard at a high rate in 1925 is seen as a major contribution to the severity of the Depression. Trust in the gold-backed paper money also led to an aggressive programme of international lending by the dominant currencies, with Britain lending £100 million from 1800 to 1825 alone. The loans were followed by a string of defaults: Mexico 1824, Columbia 1826, Honduras 1827, Argentina 1832, Portugal 1832, and many others throughout the century. Even the high point of stability in the mid twentieth century saw a number of defaults, including Turkey, Chile, Argentina and Brazil (Rowbotham 2000: 34). Britain came off the gold standard finally in 1931 and the US stopped exchanging currency for gold to anyone except central banks in 1933. It was this final central bank 'window' that was formally abolished in 1973.

A second version of the gold standard, a gold exchange standard, emerged from the Bretton Woods agreement of 1944. Exchange rates were set against the dollar, which in turn was anchored to gold at the rate of $35 dollars an ounce. However, as Wray argues, the 'goldbugs' have got it the wrong way around: 'it was not gold that gave money its value but rather gold had money value because its price was pegged in terms of money by the public authorities' (2012: 263). He goes on to point out that the two centuries of gold standard were not stable. In the US it saw 'periodic fluctuations and deep depressions, with major financial panics and crises every couple of decades' (2012: 264). D'Arista agrees that 'it was actually sterling credit and capital markets in London – not gold – that underpinned the system' (2009: 636). However, what the gold standard did represent was the power of dominant currencies, first the pound and then the dollar. The formal abandonment of the gold standard in 1973 did not remove from the US the 'exorbitant privilege' of being the world's reserve currency, a concept attributed to the French politician, Valery Giscard d'Estaing (Eichengreen 2011: 4).

Reserve Currencies and Exorbitant Privilege

The 'exorbitant privilege' is one of seigniorage. As on the national level, the privilege of being able to create and circulate a world currency brings the benefit of first use. When the US took over the British role of reserve currency it had large reserves of gold and had not experienced domestic ravages from two world wars. The US became the world's leading economy with a comfortable surplus of international trade. This allowed it to make generous loans for postwar reconstruction under the Marshall Plan, with the expectation that the money would return as payment for US products. However, as war-torn countries scrambled back onto their feet the US trading privilege began to erode. Far from being the world's major lender and producer, the US eventually became the world's leading consumer. Nevertheless the dollar still retained its privilege as the leading reserve currency.

Since the suspension of the gold standard in 1971, all currencies have been fiat currencies, that is, they rest on social, public and commercial trust alone; there is not even a mythical anchor. The international monetary world is composed of 'hard' and 'soft' currencies, those that carry international authority and those that don't. The abolition of the gold standard did not undermine the dollar as the world's main reserve currency, even though it was no longer convertible to gold. There are challengers, most notably the euro, but its poor design and consequent difficulties have undermined its seeming potential. The pound has had its day, the yen is undermined by the long Japanese recession, and the Chinese renminbi is yet to show its hand. Before the crisis, around two thirds of the world's foreign reserves were held in dollars, around a quarter in euros and under 5 per cent in pounds and yen. China remains the main holder of dollars.

Being the world's banker has both benefits and penalties for the US economy. As countries want to hold dollars they provide goods and services to the US without demanding goods and services in return. As a consequence, the US can run a large balance of payments deficit. This could make it vulnerable to a speculative attack, but as countries would not want to see their holdings of dollars devalue it is not in their interest to undermine the dollar – they are in a 'dollar trap' (Prasad 2014). The US also benefits from many dollar holders wanting to invest in US sovereign debt, seeing it as one of the safest investments in a time of financial instability. The weakness of the US position is that at some point all those dollars may come home to roost. This is the 'Triffin Dilemma' whereby reserve currency countries create global liquidity through running deficits on their balance of payments, but run the risk that this will undermine their currency. The dilemma of being the world's reserve currency is that to create sufficient currency for the world to financialise, it must suffer a balance of payments problem unless it can attract a 'tsunami of foreign capital' (Varoufakis 2011: 223). As Varoufakis points out, 70 per cent of the dollar surplus from China, Germany and Japan went back to the US Treasury as public debt or to Wall Street (2011: 223). In either case, it represented a financial investment, not a purchase of goods and non-financial services. The money has only temporarily returned, and while it may solve the balance of payments problem, it does not help bridge the deficit in trade. Varoufakis sees the US as the first modern Global Minotaur, 'a terrible beast that stabilised an unstable world' (2011: 225). It led two hegemonic eras that were both brought down by the money system. The first gold standard era was more benign because America dominated the global economy as the major producer, not the major consumer. Most importantly, the US recycled its earnings through postwar dollar aid. This collapsed when new trading surplus countries emerged (Germany, Japan and now China) which did not recycle their surplus. As a result, the US went into deficit, which was compounded by the Vietnam war. This first era of US domination was relatively successful because it was based on 'a global surplus recycling mechanism' not 'vulgar exploitation' (Varoufakis 2011: 22).

A 'global hegemon' can survive if it has a balance of payments surplus through trading. That is, as in the first era, if the creator of the global dominant reserve currency is also the world's dominant trader. It can then create and circulate currency and re-earn it through exports. The problem comes when it can no longer re-earn the currency and has to raise interest rates to attract it back. This strengthens the currency which undermines exports still further. Devaluation would help make exports more competitive, but this would undermine the strength of the currency as a world money. In either situation, there needs to be a monetary recycling mechanism for the global hegemon to reissue or reclaim the dominant currency. It is this that the German-dominated Eurozone lacks. It operates under the 'absurd pretence' that a currency union can prosper without a surplus recycling mechanism (Varoufakis 2011: 224). With monetary dominance comes monetary responsibility, something the leading economy of the Eurozone has to learn.

The second hegemonic era Varoufakis identifies is the current one of floating exchange rates and the rapid expansion of globalisation and financialisation. Although flawed, the gold standard did allow individual nations some control over exchange rates and the movement of finance. The privatisation of the money supply and the loss of public control of money systems in the second era means that finance capitalism is able 'to print *global private money* at will' (Varoufakis 2011: 223, emphasis in the original). The US financial sector as the 'custodian' of global financialisation became so profligate that it nearly bankrupted global finance. The irony was that the global financial system was so badly damaged that money poured back into the two countries most responsible for the mess, the US and the UK, because they had sovereign currencies. All the austerity scare stories of the 'money markets' driving up interest rates for their sovereign debt were unfounded. However the global hegemon may not escape the Triffin Dilemma; the US may not be able to continue to benefit from its 'exorbitant privilege' without undermining its own domestic priorities (D'Arista and Erturk 2010: 62).

During the gold standard era, commercial banks exchanged foreign exchange with their own central bank. These then settled with other central banks. When the fixed interest rate regime broke down, commercial banks settled international payments directly using a reserve currency. This undermined the central bank's ability to control the cross-border movement of finance capital.

Multiple Currencies

One possible solution to break the power of the 'global hegemon' is to have a number of competing reserve currencies. However, this might compound rather than solve the problem if powerful currencies vie with each other to maximise their 'exorbitant privilege', or form into large opposed trading blocs (Wheatley 2013: 151). Multiple reserve currencies would also not solve the problem of the weaker currencies. In order to get access to the global economy, they would still need to establish a stable relationship with one or more of the stronger currencies. One solution is to 'peg' their currency to a stronger one through adopting a fixed exchange rate. This requires sufficient holdings of the stronger currency to honour the convertibility of the weaker currency at that rate. The limitation of a peg is that it is hard to maintain and, as Argentina found, speculators can force devaluation. This can lead to a run on the stronger currency reserves while debts held in that currency are more expensive to service. This loss of monetary sovereignty is the reason that MMT calls for all sovereign currencies to adopt floating exchange rates rather than pegs or other links to stronger currencies. It argues that no sovereign country should be monetarily constrained by the economic decisions of another country.

However, even if weaker countries control their own currency, they can only trade using the stronger currency. Often they have to borrow these currencies rather than earn them. This makes them susceptible to changing exchange rates and interest rates. This was the position that led to the Third World Debt Crisis. As discussed earlier, a combination of stagflation, finance from oil revenues and the privatisation of the money supply led to ample money but a lack of profitable opportunities in the older economies. The money found ready takers in the newly developing countries. Many majority nations that had recently been liberated from colonialism were keen to modernise their economies, create prestige projects as well as build up their military forces. In fact, many experienced coups and had become military regimes. Corruption and lack of democratic accountability meant that autocratic leaders funded lavish lifestyles or diverted money to off-shore personal accounts.

Often the original loans were made at relatively cheap interest rates. However within ten years, as monetarist theory replaced Keynesianism, interest rates rose sharply. Many countries found themselves with unsustainable debt, among other adverse conditions such as falling commodity prices. Repayments began to outstrip the original loan schedules. Countries found themselves having to apply to the IMF for rescue and then suffer the pain of 'structural adjustment' – forerunner of the austerity programmes now demanded by neoliberal economic ideology. All the impact of floating currencies and changing interest rates was placed upon the debtor country, compounding the problem of global inequality and poverty. On the grounds that many of these debts were 'odious' because they were corrupt or unfair, campaigners eventually managed to get some loans to the poorest countries cancelled. However, much of the debt had been sold to so-called 'debt vultures' who demanded payment of the whole original sum.

The advent of multiple reserve currencies would not resolve the problems of global inequality. It might even create global instability and conflict as the privatisation of public currencies and their dispersal around the world could create monetary competition between sovereign states, even a new mercantilism. Like the original mercantilism, will warships follow where traders lead?

A New Mercantilism?

The original mercantilism saw the struggle to obtain precious metals and the spoils of trade forge a close relationship between trade and war (Mellor 2014). Today, instead of fighting each other to accumulate gold, countries are competing to accumulate leading currencies (Rickards 2011). At one level, countries using and holding each other's currencies could be seen as a good thing, fulfilling the promise of neo-liberalism by turning the world into one large economy. On the other hand, a nation's currency reflects a potential call on its labour and resources. Holding a nation's currency is very different from holding gold, which is a commodity in itself that does not necessarily reflect a debt or obligation to honour. A fiat currency (i.e. a currency not made of, or backed by, a commodity of equivalent intrinsic value) is a promise, a claim. As with all fiat currencies, the backing for that promise is the labour, goods, services, resources and possessions of the people in whose name that currency was issued.

Globalisation and financialisation depend on the honouring of public currencies if profit is to be realised and accumulated. Given that globalised trading and finance has produced almost unlimited amounts of money designated in national currencies, it is the people in those nations who will have to honour that debt. Once again, it is the public collectively who have to honour the outcomes of the private creation and manipulation of public currency. This is the message of the financial crisis; the people have had to pay in austerity for the domestic and global activities of privatised finance. Their wages and benefits are being cut and they are being asked to privatise their national assets. Both the domestic and the global arena depend on social trust and public authority of monetary arrangements. What would happen if that trust broke down? The first wave of mercantilism saw the militarisation of commercial activities, and it is not without note that the leading global currency is created by the leading military nation.

Imbalances in trade and the global flow of capital mean that while some countries are mired in sovereign debt, others have built substantial surpluses of foreign exchange. Countries with major natural resources or high levels of production are storing up reserves of other currencies, particularly the dollar. This has led to the growth of international investment not just by commercial companies but also by states, through the proliferation of sovereign wealth funds. These have been used to buy up resources, land, infrastructure and financial assets around the world. Those countries running a deficit in reserve currencies are particularly vulnerable.

A substantial portion of dollar currency reserves is held by China, which has reinvested much of this in US government debt, but it has also built up several sovereign wealth funds. Among primary exporters, per capita, Norway has become one of the wealthiest countries in the world. Its sovereign wealth fund is composed of taxes on oil and gas and dividends from public ownership of the oil and gas industry. Funds have also been established by many Middle East states. Some of these came to the rescue of western banks in the early stages of the crisis and lost a great deal of money.

As was the case for the original mercantilism, is there a potential source of conflict in modern mercantilism? Could this occur if one sovereign state owned a strategic asset such as an airport or invested in a sensitive technology in another state? The US has already blocked deals such as the proposed purchase of its ports. Equally, conflict could occur if a deficit nation refused to offer suitable investment for the substantial surplus of its currency that had been accumulated by another nation. Conflict has already occurred over monetary spheres of influence. One trigger of the Iraq war was held to be Saddam Hussein's decision to price oil in euros. Blocking access to dollar clearing was also a major sanction against Iran. Currency has long been an agent of war: 'before US-led forces invaded Afghanistan in 2001, the CIA smoothed the path by buying the loyalty of warlords with suitcases and knapsacks full of crisp US$100 bills' (Wheatley 2013: 9). Wheatley also points out that Wellington could pay his way with Bank of England notes, whereas Napoleon had to use gold. Fiat money was also stronger than gold during the Dutch independence struggle against Spain, as the Dutch 'could always use their credit to buy mercenary armies year after year ... against the Spanish which had no credit (despite) its access to gold in the new world' (Wheatley 2013: 18).

If the aim is to avoid conflict, it would seem unwise to have a global monetary system based on the competitive accumulation of currency or the use of money in an aggressive way. A more benign international monetary regime is needed. The world's current monetary system is 'incompatible with full employment objectives ... deepens inequality ... destroy[s] people's livelihoods and [is] accompanied by severe environmental degradation' (Nadal 2011: 171). The principles of sufficiency and use value would be less likely to lead to conflict than the search for growth and profit. It would be impossible to avoid all global trade as resources are not evenly distributed, climates differ and new technologies are invented that need to be shared. The question then becomes how to get the best out of international provisioning systems, while reducing the potential for destruction and conflict, particularly given the possibility of an ever-increasing scramble for resources in a resource-limited world (Panayotakis 2011).

Neither the gold standard nor floating exchange rates have shown a capacity to enable global provisioning on a sufficiency basis. Floating exchange rates have also driven the huge growth in financial derivatives. The proposition of MMT, that floating exchange rates are necessary to achieve sovereign monetary autonomy, has already been questioned. MMT argues that governments can never fail to pay debts accrued in their own currency, as they can always create new money (monetise the debt). The case is very different if money is borrowed in another currency. This is real debt with no control over interest rates.

As the aim here is sufficiency provisioning at the global level, this is unlikely to be achieved under current conditions of floating exchange rates and dominant reserve currencies. Other solutions will need to be found.

Alternative Proposals for a Global Monetary System

Global sufficiency provisioning could only be achieved under conditions of global social justice and respect for the ecological cost of trade. Trade would need to be fair and based on necessity. Resources, climate and skills are not evenly distributed across the globe and some exchange will always be necessary. People have also always travelled to explore other cultures and geographies. Could there be a global, cross-national or international money system that would enable trade of use value and discourage trade purely for economic or monetary advantage? Using money to exchange use value could be relatively straightforward when money circulates in established communities. What would make people trust a supranational system?

Modern money theorists are right to argue that sovereign monetary systems should be autonomous. There can be no democratic control of money if there is no governance framework in which people can participate. The aim would be to find a way to organise the global money system that enables countries to participate in global trade without having to 'amass someone else's currency', where every country would be able to 'engage in trade and borrow and invest externally in its own currency' (D'Arista and Erturk 2010: 77–9). Rowbotham agrees that if all countries paid for goods in their own currency it would mean that the recipient country would need to trade in return in order to 'spend' the money (2000: 183). However, this doesn't get over the lack of balance in exchange rates. The US would still find more ready acceptance of its payment than a country with a low value currency.

Countries need to be able to interact with other currencies on the basis of equality. A priority must be parity of purchasing power. Exchange rates should not be determined by global hegemons or a global currency market, but by a rate that adjusts for equivalent domestic costs. A commodity that costs the average monthly income for someone in the US should also cost the average monthly income for someone in Bangladesh. Given the current inequality between currencies direct interaction between them is unlikely to produce such parity of outcome. Possible alternative solutions would be a common global currency that replaces existing currencies or works alongside them, or some form of buffer currency to intercede between national or regional currencies.

A Global Currency

A Report of the United Nations Commission of Experts on Reforms of the International Monetary and Financial System in 2009 argued that a new global reserve currency was an 'idea whose time had come'. It suggested exchanging national currencies for a global currency (D'Arista and Erturk 2010: 69,75). The case for a global currency is that it could avoid the problem of exchange rate gamblers and make the flow of goods and services much easier and potentially more equal, by breaking down barriers (Arestis et al. 2005: 523). Such a supranational money would replace dollars and other reserve currencies while a global central bank would clear payments, establish quotas, provide overdrafts and coordinate monetary policies (Alessandrini and Fratianni 2008: 12). The global currency would be created as 'the liability of a true world central bank that uses it to provide liquidity to other banks in a global money market' (Arestis et al. 2005: 509).

What would be the Janus-face of such a central bank? Would it be a system like the bank-led currency systems? Would the main face of the global central bank be towards the commercial banking sector, responding endogenously to global demand for public currency based on a commercial money supply? If so, this would not lead to sufficiency provisioning or exchange based on use value. Such a global central bank would not solve the problem of the necessity of public money to support a privatised debt-based money supply. Like the euro it would have only one face, towards the commercial banking sector, with all the weaknesses that entails.

A global currency would need a global financial infrastructure that could intervene politically and economically across state boundaries, and this might be hard to achieve even in the long run. The evidence of the euro shows that a banking system with no public authority behind it cannot work. A world currency would be little use without a global authority that could deal with distribution issues. The experience of the euro has shown that merely introducing a single currency does not eliminate social or geographic inequalities. For this to happen, there would need to be a global public authority to create the global currency free of debt in a redistributive way. This is the vision of Huber and Robertson who called for an international currency created by an independent international authority. Rather than just aiming to stabilise the global trading system, they argue that the newly created global money would be used directly for equitable aims. The money would be given to the UN to spend into circulation and help fund its administration. Money could also be given proportionately (i.e. on a per capita basis) to national governments as a redistributive measure, a form of international 'basic income' (Huber and Robertson 2000: 56). Huber and Robertson see this as one of many social and public money systems, from the local through the national to the global level. However, if the money system is to be democratic, the main focus must be at a more local level.

The possibility of a global currency replacing all other currencies is very remote given the experience of the euro. It would also be very difficult to have any democratic control over money supply. If the global currency operated alongside existing currencies it would be unlikely to solve the problem of inequality and the dominance of reserve currencies. It would be like the ecu before the euro, an optional currency. This would seem to indicate that the global monetary system should not be a global trading currency but a 'buffer' system, that prevents currencies directly interacting with each other.

Keynes' Bancor

The bancor was a global 'buffer' currency proposed by Keynes in the run up to the Bretton Woods meeting of 1944, called to discuss the postwar global financial arrangements (Cato 2009: 77). His ideas did not make it on to the agenda because of American pressure to use the dollar as the world's reserve currency. The hegemonic domination of the US Anglo-American model of global capitalism saw the establishment of the 'holy trinity' of the IMF, the World Bank and initially the GATT (General Agreement on Tariff and Trade) which was replaced by the WTO (World Trade Organisation). The US-dominated system has been seen as neglecting the interests of the majority world (Peet 2009). It also created, or at least did not prevent, the conditions that led to the financial crisis of 2007–8.

Keynes' proposal was to put a barrier between national currencies, that is, to have a currency of account at the global level. Keynes warned that free trade, flexible exchange rates and free movement of capital globally were incompatible with maintaining full employment at the local level. The buffer mechanism, the *bancor* (bank gold), would provide a flexible international payments system operating through an International Clearing Union. Each country would decide their own currency fix to the bancor, and limited fluctuations would be allowed. Countries would trade using the bancor and settle their accounts with it. Countries would buy bancors from an International Central Bank. The key to Keynes' system was a mechanism to balance world trade whereby both surplus and deficit economies would be penalised. To initiate the system, countries would be allocated bancors according to their previous levels of trade. This would enshrine the status quo, but unused credit balances could be reallocated. Although Keynes lost the Bretton Woods settlement to the US, Davidson argues that the US adopted the spirit of his plan:

> While exchange rates were fixed under the Bretton Woods Agreement, in the early years after the Second World War the United States avoided amassing surplus international reserves by providing grants to the war torn nations, initially via the Marshall Plan and then via other foreign aid programs. In essence, the United States accepted the Keynes Plan suggestion that it is in the best interest of all nations if the major creditor nation bears the major burden of reducing trade imbalances and international payments adjustments. (Davidson 2008: 3).

Following Keynes, Davidson has called for an International Monetary Clearing Union (IMCU) that would insulate economies from each other, but without a central bank or currency. Davidson sees the IMCU system as based on an agreed accounting unit that would become the new international reserve asset. The IMCU means of account would operate as the international standard by fiat rather than through its relationship to gold or any other scarce and valuable commodity. Only central banks would be able to access the accounting units and exchange them with other central banks. Like Keynes' proposal, 'excessively large' credit balances over time would be discouraged by the threat of elimination. This would create an incentive to spend them or transfer them to a poorer country. Overdrafts could also be provided if necessary (Davidson 2008: 300–5). Insulating currencies from each other would eliminate the opportunity for currency speculation and the inequality created by 'hard' and 'soft' currencies. It would also enable governments to monitor payments for illegal activities or tax evasion. This approach to economic sustainability would require a return to the era when governments controlled the rate of exchange of their national currency with other national currencies (Cato 2009). Davidson suggests the exchange rate of domestic currencies with the IMCU unit would be a domestically produced basket of goods to reflect purchasing power parity. Each country would fix its own local rate reflecting its own local conditions. That rate would remain in place unless there was permanent change in the domestic circum-stances. Other possible measures to create purchasing parity could be a level of wages or average income (Mellor 2010a: 174).

Richard Douthwaite has put forward a proposal for international trade to be based on a global energy-backed currency unit, or EBCU (1999: 57). Such a proposal would link two major issues: climate change and global financial instability. Monetary limits would be determined by the capacity of the planetary environment. The global currency would be issued in relation to a sustainable level of energy usage and would be allocated per capita. A global central bank would issue the Ebcus, which countries could use for trade or to buy carbon permits (Cato 2006: 35–7). The problem with such a proposal is that it puts a physical limit on the issue of money and assumes that all trade is energy using. There are certainly good reasons for curtailing world energy use, but integrating limits on consumption with the money system may be over-complicating two questions that might be better treated separately.

IMF Special Drawing Rights – A Halfway House?

A move towards an IMF currency was made in the late 1960s through the creation of Special Drawing Rights. Robert Triffin described SDRs as 'collectively created assets' that could be used to support development programmes (D'Arista 2009: 642). Under the influence of neoliberalism, however, the IMF allocated them according to IMF funding levels. One third of the SDRs went to the US and the UK. IMF does its transactions in SDRs but their use is limited because they are not convertible into local currencies.

Stiglitz and Greenwald have put forward a proposal to expand the role of SDRs to deal with the negative aspects of reserve currencies. They argue that states need to hold substantial reserve currencies to protect themselves, which can be deflationary. Reserves are mainly dollars as the US is the 'deficit of last resort' (2009: 17). As holding US Treasury bills or reserves earns little or no interest, the dollars have funded sovereign wealth funds instead. The problem with reserve currencies is that they get entangled with domestic economic priorities and are unstable and inequitable. Stiglitz and Greenwald suggest a public money solution. The IMF should issue SDRs on a substantial and regular basis as an alternative international reserve. They calculate that $200 billion annually would be sufficient, assuming international reserves at about $3,000 billion (2009: 27). The SDRs would be credited to the IMF accounts of member countries in proportion to their current IMF fund positions. To deal with problems of surplus accumulation of reserves, SDR allocations could be taxed. The taxes could then be used as a source of global financial aid to be distributed among developing countries. Stiglitz and Greenwald see the SDR reserve system as a form of co-operative mutual help. The international community would be providing help in times of crisis, allowing a country to spend beyond its means (2009: 27–8).

D'Arista has responded to an earlier version of this proposal by asking whether it escapes the power of the current reserve currencies. The aim is to create a new currency, 'global greenbacks'. These would be granted to developing countries and countries with financial difficulties. They could then be converted into hard currencies to service debts and finance imports (D'Arista 2009: 646). Also, a trust fund of conventional hard currencies would be established, to enable countries in crisis to exchange their global greenbacks. D'Arista is concerned that the proposal does not overcome the dominance of powerful countries as the trust fund would necessarily rely on them for contributions. Rather than seeing the 'greenbacks' as a supplement to existing reserve currencies, she would want to see their creation and issue as an incremental path towards an international unit of account and means of payment in the international system. She warns that whatever system develops, it must curtail the power of private finance: 'failure to do so would likely expose the reserve asset once again to the perils of speculation. Given the damage done by the process of privatising the international monetary system since the 1970s, the debate on reform must include discussions of the appropriate criteria for determining changes in exchange rates and how those determinations should be made' (2009: 647).

A Buffer Currency for Sufficiency and Social Justice

A money system that would enable democratically determined provisioning must be sovereign, as MMT rightly states. However, sovereignty is compromised if there is the need to interact with more powerful currencies. MMT is therefore wrong to envisage a system of floating exchange rates, certainly in an era of financialisation and globalisation. If all economies were based on sufficiency provisioning, floating currencies would not be a problem. That is not the case. Trade and finance are based on finding the most profitable opportunities. Production goes to the country with the cheapest labour, least tax and minimum regulation. Finance capital goes wherever there is a speculative advantage. Economic migrants take huge and expensive risks to get to a country where they can earn many times their local wages. Developing countries try to balance low prices for their exports with high prices for imports.

The aim for an international currency must be to insulate currencies from each other and create purchasing parity between nations. To insulate currencies all international exchange would need to be via the buffer currency. There would be no other currencies operating at the global level. Something that costs a month's pay in one country should cost a month's pay in another. There should be no monetary incentive to globalise production. Countries should be free to expand or contract their domestic economy without fear of exchange rate consequences. Tax havens could not operate as the money would need to be filtered through the buffer currency.

Sufficiency provisioning also means that trade would be discouraged rather than encouraged. A major problem with Keynes' proposal and its successors is that it aimed to create growth within the global economy as a response to the Great Depression. A sufficiency approach would want to see trade minimised. This could be achieved by a transaction tax every time the buffer currency was used and taxes upon transport. Existing reserves would be exchanged for the buffer currency. The buffer currency would be a public money created free of debt and either allocated to countries on an egalitarian basis or used for public purposes. Exchange rates with each domestic currency would be calculated to achieve international purchasing parity.

Given the presumption of sufficiency, global finance for global trade would not be a priority. As no country would be short of its own money there would be no reliance on foreign earnings except to balance international expenditure within the buffer currency. This does not mean that countries would be insular. People would still travel widely to share experiences and settle in other countries. There would also be trade in things that the local economy could not provide. The main change under this system, is that comparative monetary values would not be the driver. Container loads of goods would no longer pass container loads of similar goods going in the opposite direction. Most importantly it would curb the power of global speculative finance, which currently forms the lion's share of global foreign exchange.

8

Conclusion: Crisis and Change

A time of crisis provides the opportunity for change as it exposes the failures and contradictions of the established order: the chance to achieve radical momentum, or at least to undermine the prevailing hegemony. It is the argument of this book that the trigger for the 2007–8 crisis lay within the money supply. Capitalism's major weakness was its failure to understand the social and public nature of money. This led to the privatisation and commodification of money, which was socially, ecologically and economically unsustainable. As with all crises, the elements of new possibilities lie within the ashes of the existing order. The potential for change lay in the resurgence and visibility of public money; the creation of money free of debt. Reclaiming the social and public power of money can provide the foundations of a socially just and ecologically sustainable structure of provisioning.

The major contradiction of capitalist money is that the privatisation of the money supply was based on debt. This provides the 'elastic credit' capitalism needs, but is constantly threatened by implosion when the system can take no more debt. A second contradiction is the starvation of monetary resources for the public sector (handbag economics), which removes the only source of debt-free money that could sustain demand. A third is linked to the second. Starving the public sector of money undermines the political legitimacy of the system. Disaffection with poor public services and conspicuous private wealth breeds cynicism and discontent. However, the right, rather than the left, may be the beneficiary of popular dissent if there is no convincing radical alternative.

There needs to be an engagement with the neglected critique of money if this opportunity is not to be lost. Failure to see money as an active economic agent removes the chance to build action around money as the means of achieving social change. Theories of money, such as those drawn on in this book, have been around for more than a century. Many books and papers have been published for academic and general audiences. Optimistically, there is evidence that this analysis is beginning to take root with a groundswell of debate and discussion. For example, in 2012 the IMF published a paper that links contemporary monetary theories with earlier advocates of an active public monetary role in response to the Great Depression. If mainstream organisations are beginning to tentatively rethink the structure of the money supply in a public direction, this must be an opportunity for the left to make the case for prioritising public and social provisioning through the democratisation of public money.

This book identifies three avenues to radical change. First, it opens up a path to economic democracy, sustainability and social justice through the democratisation of money. It provides a clear alternative to the market fundamentalism of TINA ('there is no alternative'). It also provides an alternative economic framework to command economies on the Soviet model. It is both democratic and flexible. It is not, however, some fudge of a 'third way' (Giddens 2000). There is no compromise between economic democracy and the market. Priority must go to the social and public economy (social and public provisioning), with the remaining commercial market in a secondary role. The democratisation of money is not about bringing commercial values into public provisioning. Quite the opposite: democratically determined public values would drive the commercial sector.

Second, the book has shown that this is no utopian dream. The mechanism of public control already exists in the form of public money. This has been defined as the creation of the public currency by public monetary authorities. Moreover, it has been argued that public money, free of debt, is vital to the functioning of the current privatised money system. The commercial banking sector has privatised the supply of public currency, but it cannot sustain that supply without public backing.

Third, the experience of the 2007–8 crisis has demonstrated the dependency of the private sector on public money. Awareness of this contradiction can make a major contribution to radical politics and economics. The analysis and critique of money is not a diversion from the struggle against capitalism, it is a core aspect of it. Without the socially and publicly constructed mechanism of money, capitalism cannot realise its profit. Control of the money supply is therefore vital to capitalism. Challenging that control is as important as challenging the ownership and control of other factors of production. While there are mounting critical analyses of money, and many advocates of innovation and reform, these have not gone to the heart of radical critiques of capitalism. Lack of awareness of the politics of money has strengthened TINA's hand. There is No Alternative because the possibility of change is removed by a deadening monetary ideology, identified here as 'handbag economics'. This book has framed the debate in terms of a choice between the commodification and privatisation of the supply of public currency as debt, and the democratic control of public money, free of debt, as the means of sufficiency provisioning.

Privatised Money and Public Penury

In modern economies, the privatised supply of the public currency through bank loans has become a major source of money. The important difference between a privatised money supply and a public money supply is debt. While privatised money can *only* be based on debt, public money *can* be created and circulated debt free. An example is quantitative easing. Money has been created out of 'thin air' by central banks and used to purchase financial assets. The money was not borrowed from anyone or lent to anyone. There was no public outcry at this blatant example of 'printing money' for the benefit of the financial sector, because control of the public currency is not on the political agenda.

Without recognition of the vital role of public money, the commercial role of central banks can continue what is effectively a form of money laundering. What was originally a process of commercial liability for commercially issued private money has put the nation's public credit in place of that of commercial banks. This is because private credit is being laundered as public currency. It has turned privatised money supply into public money supply and private liability into public liability. The stance of handbag economics that the state must not create money is entirely hypocritical. The privatised world of money commodified as debt could not function without a publicly created money supply. Under the guise of 'credit' the financial sector is creating the public currency and issuing it largely to itself.

As noted above, the contradiction of debt as a source of the money supply is that it is unsustainable. If the willingness to lend or borrow dries up, so does the supply of public currency. Supplying new money based on debt gives the most reckless borrowers disproportionate power over the direction of the economy. Money supply also shifts towards the most speculative risk-takers, increasing inequality. The era of financialised capitalism has seen a vast increase in both inequality and money supply. This led to a casino capitalism that made little material contribution to goods and services, while miring people in debt. Conventional theory makes the assumption that central banks can constrain or encourage commercial bank lending. This proved unfounded as banks poured out loans in the boom before the crisis and failed to make loans in the recession. At the same time, central banks had to provide unlimited support.

In 2014 Oxfam reported that since the advent of neoliberalism in the 1980s there had been a global explosion of inequality, with only a slight pause when China industrialised. Political campaigns focused on the top 1 per cent where wealth was concentrated, taking inequality in Britain back to the levels before the First World War (Dorling 2014, Weeks 2014). The 1 per cent did not even carry out the basic capitalist task of generating employment through investment in productive industry (Sayer 2014). Instead, their wealth was derived from unearned income: dividends, capital gains, interest and rent. The rich syphoned off their wealth through tax havens, while dominating both politics and economic life.

Despite studies arguing that inequality was bad for capitalism (Piketty 2014), and bad for people (Wilkinson and Pickett 2010), nothing appeared to change, 'the establishment' was still firmly in place (Jones 2014). As Naomi Klein (2014) argued with regard to climate change, the opportunity was not taken to move economies in a different direction. Bankers and businesses were rescued, but not the people or the planet. The market assumption that wealth would trickle down had failed, the 'experiment' in neoliberalism had not worked (Bowman and Froud 2014). The capitalist financial system has not even performed well within its own terms. A study of the US over a 150-year time span (1860–2010) found there was no apparent relationship between the share of national income going to the financial sector and the rate of economic growth (Epstein 2013: 87–8).

As Wolfgang Streeck (2014) has argued, the dominance of the financial sector and the growth of debt are setting up a conflict between democracy and capitalism. In particular, the tax system is failing and the public infrastructure with it. The 'tax state' of the post Second World War era generated manageable budget deficits, balanced corporate-union power, and enabled uncontentious government expenditure. As this book has discussed, rather than being able to create its own money and tax its people, the modern state has become a debtor to the commercial banking system and the financial sector generally. This then becomes a justification for austerity. Debt-based money creation compounds the social, ecological and economic problems that David Harvey sees as the three most dangerous contradictions of capitalism. These are: that capital is always accumulating faster than opportunities for profitable investment; what growth there is threatens the survival of the environment; and the social impact of recurrent capitalist crises may eventually prove unacceptable to the mass of the population (Harvey 2014: 264). As both Streeck and Harvey point out, debt as the foundation of the money supply and public spending is incompatible with democracy.

Money for the People

Democratising the public currency would provide the framework for an ecologically sustainable and socially just means of provisioning human communities. To focus on the monetary system is not to ignore other targets of social and ecological critique, but it has powerful resonance in the context of the 2007–8 financial crisis. What the crisis revealed was the frailty of the current privatised money and banking systems and their reliance on public monetary authorities. The private sector turned out not to be so private after all. At the heart of capitalist realisation and accumulation of profit lies the social trust and public authority of the public currency. This book has shown the intertwined nature of the public and private systems of money and banking.

As the Mexican economist Alejandro Nadal argues, economic priorities are not set by some natural law; they reflect political choices. How money is created and used by different types of agents has 'profound macroeconomic implications in terms of growth and stability' (2011: 145). The ecological crises facing economies today are a consequence of the 'privatisation of one of economics' most important public domains, the dimension of money creation ... Does it make sense to run the banking system through private agents seeking profits when we are discussing sustainability objectives?' (2011: 148–9).

The choice between debt and democracy sets a privatised money supply based on money created as debt against a public money supply free of debt, where priorities are set by democratic debate. As pointed out earlier, public control here should not be assumed to be the same as state or government control. As it is the public collectively who underpin the money system, it is the public at all levels who should determine how money is created and circulated. As public money is free of debt at the point of creation, it could be spent, lent or allocated into the economy at the local, national or global level. Proposals were made in Chapter 3 for how such a system could operate.

Taking debt out of the money supply would enable both sufficiency and ecological sustainability. It would remove the destructive growth dynamic inherent in the present commercial money supply. Money would not need to be returned with interest. It would allow money to be allocated on the basis of need, not greed. Democracy would mean reclaiming public control of money and using it for publicly determined ends. This would end the need to accumulate public debt. In fact, surplus public expenditure (deficit) should be welcomed as it creates money that can circulate without being reclaimed as tax or debt repayment.

In Praise of Deficit (Surplus Expenditure)

There is no reason why a public expenditure deficit should become a public debt. A deficit merely means that more money has been circulated than has been reclaimed, that is, there has been surplus expenditure. A debt means that money has been borrowed. The main ideological victory of neoliberalism has been to make the public sector seem dependent upon the private sector's capacity to create and circulate money, whereas the opposite is true. The private sector could not exist without public money. A deficit is not a debt but a surplus. It is a surplus of currency created over the amount of currency collected. It increases the number of monetary obligations/entitlements in circulation. This increases provisioning capacity. More people are rewarded for the goods and services they provide, or have entitlement to access those that they need. In the same way that an elastic supply of credit and debt enabled the production and accumulation of private wealth, the elastic supply of public deficits/surpluses could enable the expansion of public provision and public wealth.

Surplus public expenditure need not be seen as a deficit or a debt. The decision to do so is ideological. There is some justification in selling sovereign debt as a monetary instrument, but other more direct ways could be used. The creation and circulation of public money free of debt is also not any more or less inflationary than banks creating money. What is important is the capacity of the economy to provide goods and services. Whatever the source of new money, there is always the possibility of undersupply or oversupply. While undersupply can be met by new money creation, oversupply can be met by increased taxation. As discussed earlier, it has been drummed into contemporary thinking that public 'printing money' must create inflation. But examples such as Weimar Germany are both misleading and exceptional. Public money creation will not be inflationary if it increases the level of goods and services delivered and is balanced with appropriate taxation where necessary.

For the currently unpaid labour of 'women's work' and community care to receive acknowledgement of its use value in public currency, or for a citizens' income to be paid, there would need to be a large new issue of public currency. The question then becomes how much to retrieve in tax or fees. Retrieving the money through taxation would enable expenditure to be directed to those most in need and taxation to be imposed on those least in need. By contrast, to sell the deficit as a debt would mean that the public as a whole would become indebted to those wealthy enough to buy the debt. Taxation is therefore much preferable as it is progressive. The losers would be financial institutions that rely on public debt as a safe investment for their largely better off pensioners and investors. However, if there were a sufficiency provisioning public economy, there would be no need to have vast pension and insurance schemes.

Handbag Economics: Cutting the Purse Strings

This book has exposed many of the myths about money within conventional economics. Most of them come down to one simple notion: money is a limited resource. Public expenditure is particularly constrained by this claim. Every penny or cent spent in the public sector is seen as a drain on the 'productive' sector or as leading to less in the pocket of the taxpayer. Handbag economics backs this up by an appeal to commonsense. For the ordinary person it is a truism. Every individual can only spend what is in their handbag, purse or wallet. This amount can be expanded by borrowing, but that only stores up problems for the future. This 'commonsense' breaks down when the handbag analogy is applied to the public sector. It demands that the 'state' must not spend more than it receives in income. It must balance its budget and not borrow, as this puts a cost on to future generations. The 'state' here is set apart from the people, who are assumed to be on the side of the 'taxpayer'. Welfare beneficiaries are derided as lazy and undeserving, scroungers and cheats. By a sleight of hand, handbag economics has turned the people against themselves, using lies about money as the weapon.

While it is true that people individually face monetary limits, sovereign states and banks are in a very different position. They are creators as well as users of money. There is no limit to how much they can create, should they choose to do so. There are no physical limits to money creation such as precious metal supplies. Even the link of public currency with gold was ideological and expedient. As has been argued, precious metal money was historically linked to rulers; commercial banking was mainly based on private lending and personal credit. While rulers or public monetary authorities continued to control the creation of coinage and later public bank notes, a critical change occurred when bank lending subsumed the private promise on the part of the bank with the promise of the public currency. Loans were created as public currency not private promises.

This was the critical point at which public and private money became intertwined, leading to the confusion in modern money systems. Money itself has become Janus-faced; it is both public and private. If the bank cannot honour its pledges, the public will demand that the public monetary authorities make recompense; something they would not demand for other industries. When the commercial banks designate their loans in public currency, they are placing the credit-worthiness of the whole monetary nation in place of their own capital wealth. If the authorities refuse to honour that money, or cannot do so, the public currency will be under threat. For this reason, Martin Wolf and Felix Martin see bankers as effectively civil servants, but without the public service ethos or sense of public responsibility. The private creation of the public currency is ultimately a debt upon the public, while the benefit of access to that money is privatised. It is this dependence of the public on the commercial banking sector to create the public currency that must be removed.

The public sector is not a household and the private sector is not the sole creator of wealth, in terms of the provision of goods and services. The main restriction on the public sector at present is the ideological control of the money supply by the private sector. To cut the purse strings, the public sector must reclaim the monopoly of public money creation. This would then clearly differentiate the two circuits of money.

Creating Money: The Two Circuits

In Chapter 3, two circuits of money were identified: the commercial and the public. Formally, the only authority mandated to create the public currency is the public sector, the Treasury and/or the central bank. In practice, in a country like Britain, most of the public currency is created through bank lending. While public currency is usually taken to mean notes and coin, this book includes money created electronically or on paper records. The idea that bank accounts are a different form of money from public sector money (credit money as against high powered money) is rejected. When banks make new loans they are creating new public currency. The important difference is the way in which it is created: as debt or free of debt. While bank-created currency is always created through loans, publicly created money can be circulated free of debt. It is the latter public money that is the focus of this book: public currency created by public authority free of debt at the point of creation.

It has been argued here that the public circuit creates and spends money, some or all of which is then demanded back as tax, or taken in fees or payments. This circuit generally puts more money into circulation than it extracts. It is this surplus expenditure that is described as a deficit by handbag economics. The commercial circuit starts with a loan, which is eventually paid back with interest. This circuit always aims to extract more money than it circulates. As public currency flows through the economy, how the creation and circulation of money is perceived depends upon where the circuits are observed.

The private circuit flows from bank-created money lent into circulation which then appears in bank accounts as deposits (unless it is taken as cash which must be bought from the central bank) and then eventually returned with interest by the original borrower. If the circuit is observed at the point of the original loan it can be demonstrated that there is no actual transfer of money (no depositor's account is debited). If, however, the circuit is observed at the point of deposit by those the borrower has paid with the loan, as for example the seller of a car, it may appear that the new deposit starts the circuit. Equally, there is a public circuit. Public money is created and spent and later reclaimed through taxation. If the circuit is observed at the point of tax collection it would be assumed that the tax intake made the public expenditure possible. If the circuit is observed at the point of expenditure, before the tax take is secured, then the public sector is clearly creating new money.

The Central Bank: Pivot Between the Circuits

The public and private money circuits are brought together in the central bank. This was described as a confusing Janus-faced organisation, which can be a public or private institution, with both a public and private role. As a public body, the central bank has the traditional power of the ruling authority to create the public currency free of debt. As a bank, it has the commercial power to create public currency as loans. In both cases the public currency is created out of nothing (by fiat, authority alone). How it circulates this money is dependent on the political and ideological climate.

If the central bank is seen in a purely commercial context, its job is to be the bank of bankers. It holds the reserves of those banks and clears payments between them. When banks run out of reserves and can no longer get credit from other banks, the central bank is the lender of last resort. As seen during the crisis, it must make as much currency available as the bloated banking system requires. The crisis showed that no matter how irresponsible the banking and financial sector, in the last resort it falls back on the capacity of public monetary authorities to create public money. The privatised money supply also relies on the public's confidence in monetary governance.

Under handbag economics the central bank uses the sovereign right to create money to rescue the banking sector, but turns its commercial face towards the public sector. Rather than creating new money free of debt to fund the public sector, it deems the money as being borrowed. This Janus-faced nature of the central bank reflects its role as banker to the banks and banker to the state. Traditionally rulers monopolised the creation of the public currency to their personal benefit. If this was carried through into modern democracies, the central bank would create public currency for public use, for public benefit. Instead, it treats the public sector as if it were an individual borrower. Like a commercial bank, it will circulate new money only as a loan. This denies the capacity of public creation of money without debt. As a result, modern states have accumulated extensive national debts. Even when the Bank of England bought back a large portion of the outstanding public debt in its £375 billion quantitative easing programme, this debt was not cancelled. The public sector still owed it to the public central bank. This is because the evolution of modern monetary systems is incomplete.

The Unfinished History of Money

The history of money can be understood through a Marxian framework of historical epochs and contradictions. For money, the

190

epochs are traditional, autocratic and capitalist. The final stage would be the socialisation of money through democratic control. Modern money has not transcended its history, it has embodied it as social acceptance and custom, public authority and commercial promise. A major weakness of capitalism is not to realise the importance of all three aspects of money.

Nearly all societies have had some form of token (clay tablet, stick), object (shell, cattle, grain) or concept (hieroglyph) that can accord relative value. These were mainly used for tribute and other obligations, or to settle social disputes such as injury payments. This evidence has undermined the myth of conventional economics that money emerged from commerce and was based on precious metal. However, coinage was central to the emergence of autocratic rule in Europe. It was important for the conquest of land and peoples most particularly in Greece and Rome. Coinages became associated with particular centres of power. However, other forms of money were equally important, such as tally sticks or paper.

Central to the power of the ruling elites, as the state theory of money argues, is the ability to create or nominate forms of money. This power continues to the present day, but has largely been vested in a more or less independent central bank. The importance of the power to create money is that the creator has the benefit of first use of that money (seigniorage), without any obligation to repay in kind. The sovereign power to create and circulate money is also linked to the sovereign power to tax. Rather than relying on tribute in kind, goods and services could be rewarded with money. The money could then be reclaimed through taxation or other forms of payment. However, constant conflict weakened the monetary power of rulers and control of money increasingly fell into the hands of the newly emerging economic elite, as rulers became increasingly dependent on borrowing in the new form of money: commercial promises.

Commercial money emerged from the promises that traders and investors made to each other. These would sometimes be settled in coinage, but at the heart of commercial money were verbal or written promises. Fear that monarchical power was being replaced by commercial control of money is illustrated by opposition to the Bank of England from supporters of the old monarchical order, who saw the control of money passing to a 'republic of commerce'. The bourgeois revolution, largely based on paper money, broke down the old monetary order. Control of coinage tended to remain with rulers and states, but it became increasingly less important. The money system also embraced wider sectors of the economy as subsistence production and feudal labour were replaced by wage labour and investment in profit-seeking activities. A contradiction of capitalism was that while a trusted money system was essential to trade, the realisation of profits and the accumulation of wealth, there was not enough coinage to do business and the private paper money could not be trusted.

The solution to the regular collapse of commercial banks was to replace privately created monetary promises with state money, the public currency. This was the final capture of public authority. The creation of public currency was no longer confined to the state and its capacity to create money free of debt. Banks were creating public currency through their capacity to make loans. However, creating the public currency as loans opened up a new contradiction that weakened both the public and private monetary systems. States lost control of the money supply, while the public authority for money that capitalism required was compromised. The public sector became dependent upon money creation in the private sector, but the only source of new public currency was now debt.

This meant that the social, public and commercial aspects of money had been brought together in the public currency. The question then became, who was ultimately responsible for the currency: the commercial sector or the public sector? Various forms of ideology came to the rescue. Economic theory claimed that bank-created debt wasn't really money, it was only 'credit money'. Only the state produced 'real money'. This claim was undermined by handbag economics' denial of the right of the public sector to create money. This dilemma was resolved by deeming central banks to be 'independent'.

As was clear from the 2007–8 crisis, the only source of stability for the currency was the public sector. The opportunity arose for the public to reassert its sovereignty and its seigniorage; this time not as autocratic rulers, but as a democratic republic (Barry 2012). This did not happen because of two important defensive powers of capitalism: its overwhelming control of economic forces and its hegemonic ideology. The Janus-faced central banks obscured the true source of the public rescue. It was presented as a technical matter, a 'higher' level of bank lending, not the capacity of the public sector to create new money. If the people are to take control of their public currency, they will need to assert its social and public origins. The sovereignty of money needs to be passed from the capitalist class to the people. The capitalist market wrested control of money creation from the sovereign, but then harnessed it for itself. Money was privatised, not liberated.

Democratisation of monetary creation would return to the public the benefits of seigniorage. The public would have a monetary right to the products of public wealth. The people could fund themselves, to provision themselves. Under capitalist privatisation, the public currency has only valued those provisioning activities that produce a profit in money terms. Socially necessary provisioning was denigrated as a drain on the profit-creating sector. The privatisation of the money supply denied the public the use of public currency. It denied a public right to livelihood: to provisioning through the exchange of use value rather than commodity value. Under capitalism the public currency creates no requirement on the part of commercial creators of money to ensure equality of access to the means of livelihood and exchange, and thereby sustenance. The sovereign right to create money free of the need to repay has been lost for the modern public. Instead most countries are burdened with a national debt.

Cutting off the supply of commercially created public currency in favour of all money being publicly created would choke off *a* key mechanism, if not *the* key mechanism, of capital accumulation. Reclaiming the capacity to create public currency without it needing to be repaid and using it initially for public purposes would also remove public dependency on the private financial sector as exemplified by handbag economics. It would also expose how dependent the seeming profitability of the private sector is on the ability to commercially create new public currency. Money needs to complete its political revolution. The public needs to recognise that the public currency is theirs, because the only thing that 'backs' it is the people themselves. Money must be reclaimed as a Commons, subject to a commons regime of democratically determined use. New money should be created and used for the benefit of the public as a whole and not be created as debt through the banking sector. The final democratisation of money needs to take place.

Democratising money would not, of itself, destroy existing patterns of ownership and control. It would only be one link in a chain of changes needed to create socially just and ecologically sustainable communities. However, it is a major link because public money is already in public hands, evidently so following the crisis. What is needed is the political will to recognise the potential power of public money creation. At the same time, the critique of handbag economics and privatised money supply must also be framed within the wider critique of capitalism. While capitalist finance based on credit can be curtailed through returning the money supply to public control this does not in itself challenge finance capital, or capitalism itself, although it takes away a major source of its fuel.

The crisis has provided empirical evidence of the centrality of public money and the monetary malfunctioning of capitalism. What is missing is a political agent, a countervailing power to Capital. This agent must be the many voices across the globe raised in protest and widespread social unrest. These voices are in the streets, but also in governments. Poverty and the impact of austerity are major factors, but so too is debt. At present the indebted people in the more prosperous economies do not identify with the excluded poor. Yet both are the victims of neoliberal, handbag economics. Those campaigning for sufficiency of provisioning are complemented by those looking for a way out of overwork and debt peonage. This is the choice between debt and democracy. It is the choice between a privatised money system based on debt, for which the public is ultimately responsible, and a debt-free, democratically controlled money system as the framework for socially just and ecologically sustainable sufficiency provisioning.

Bibliography

All online sources last accessed July 2015

Affleck, Arthur and Mary Mellor (2006) 'Community Development Finance: A neo-market solution to social exclusion?', *Journal of Social Policy* 35:2, pp. 303–19.

Alesina, Alberto and Silvia Ardagna (2009) 'Large Changes in Fiscal Policy: Taxes Versus Spending', *National Bureau of Economic Research*, Working Paper No. 15438.

Alessandrini, P. and M. Fratianni (2008) 'Resurrecting Keynes to Revamp the International Monetary System', Working Paper, http://dea2.univpm.it/quaderni/pdf/310.pdf

Arestis, Philip and Malcolm Sawyer (2010) 'A New Paradigm for Macroeconomic Policy', Paper presented at Middlesex University, 3 December 2010, http://www.mdx.ac.uk/Assets/arestis_sawyer.pdf

Arestis, Philip, Santonu Basu and Sushanta Mallick (2005) 'Financial Globalisation: The need for a single currency and a global central bank', *Journal of Post-Keynesian Economics* 27:3, pp. 507–31.

Bajo, Claudia Sanchez and Bruno Roelants (2011) *Capital and the Debt Trap: Learning From Co-operatives in the Global Crisis*, Basingstoke: Palgrave Macmillan.

Barbier, Edward B. (2010) *A Global Green New Deal: Rethinking the Economic Recovery*, Cambridge: Cambridge University Press.

Barry, John (2012) *The Politics of Actually Existing Unsustainability*, Oxford: Oxford University Press.

Bellofiore, Riccardo (2013) 'A Heterodox Structural Keynesian: Honouring Augusto Graziani', *Review of Keynesian Economics* 1:4, pp. 425–30.

Benes, Jaromir and Michael Kumhof (2012) *The Chicago Plan Revisited*, IMF Working Paper WP/12/202.

Bennholdt-Thomsen, Veronika and Maria Mies (1999) *The Subsistence Perspective*, London: Zed Books.

Biesecker, Adelheid and Sabine Hofmeister (2010) 'Focus: (Re)productivity. Sustainable relations both between society and nature and between the genders', *Ecological Economics* 69, pp. 1703–11.

Bivens, Josh (2013) 'The Great Mistake: How Academic Economists and Policymakers Wrongly Abandoned Fiscal Policy', in Thomas I. Palley and Gustav A. Horn (eds) *Restoring Shared Prosperity: A Policy Agenda from Leading Keynesian Economists*, pp. 33–40, http://www.thomaspalley.com/docs/research/restoring_shared_prosperity.pdf

Blain, Bob (2014) 'The Root of United States Public and Private Debt, Told by the Pen of History', *Michigan Sociological Review* 28, pp. 70–88.

Blyth, Mark (2013) *Austerity: The History of a Dangerous Idea*, Oxford: Oxford University Press.

Botsch, Andreas (2013) 'Hypocritical Versus Hippocratic Economics', in Thomas I. Palley and Gustav A. Horn (eds) *Restoring Shared Prosperity: A Policy Agenda from Leading Keynesian Economists*, pp. 15–22, http://www.thomaspalley.com/docs/research/restoring_shared_prosperity.pdf

Bowman, Andrew and Julie Froud (eds) (2014) *The End of the Experiment (Manchester Capitalism)*, Manchester: Manchester University Press.

Boyle, David and Andrew Simms (2009) *The New Economics: A Bigger Picture*, London: Earthscan.

Brown, Ellen Hodgson (2013) *The Public Bank Solution: From Austerity to Prosperity*, Los Angeles: Third Millennium Press.

Cato, Molly Scott (2012) *The Bioregional Economy: Land, Liberty and the Pursuit of Happiness*, London: Routledge.

Cato, Molly Scott (2009) *Green Economics*, London: Earthscan.

Cato, Molly Scott (2006) *Market Schmarket: Building the Post-Capitalist Economy*, Cheltenham: New Clarion Press.

Chang, Ha-Joon (2014) *Economics: A User's Guide*, London: Pelican.

Chick, Victoria (1992) *On Money, Method and Keynes*, Basingstoke: Macmillan.

Chick, Victoria and Ann Pettifor (2010) *The Economic Consequences of Mr Osborne*, www.debtonation.org/wp-content/uploads/20.

Cohen, Nevin (2011) *Green Business*, Sage: London.

Colignatus, Thomas (2013) 'Money as Gold versus Money as Water', *real-world economics review* 64, pp. 90–101, http://www.paecon.net/PAEReview/issue64/Colignatus64.pdf

Cook, Richard C. (2007) 'Notes on a Return to the Gold Standard Global Research', 15 May, Http://www.globalresearch.ca/PrintArticle.php?articleId=5658

D'Arista, Jane (2009) 'The Evolving International Monetary System', *Cambridge Journal of Economics* 33, pp. 633–52.

D'Arista, Jane (2008) 'Broken Systems: Agendas for financial and monetary reform', *Report of the 17th Annual Hyman Minsky Conference*, 17–18 April, New York, www.levy.org

D'Arista, Jane and Korcut Alp Erturk (2010) 'The Case for International Monetary Reform', *real-world economics review* 55, pp. 58–81, http://www.paecon.net/PAEReview/issue55/AristaErturk55.pdf

Daly, Herman (1999) *Ecological Economics and the Ecology of Economics*, Cheltenham: Edward Elgar.

Daly, Herman (ed.) (1973) *Towards a Steady State Economy*, San Francisco: W. H. Freeman.

Davidson, Paul (2008) 'Reforming the World's International Money', *real-world economics review* 48, pp. 306–11, http://www.paecon.net/PAEReview/issue48/Davidson48.pdf

Davies, Glynn (2002) *A History of Money*, Cardiff: University of Wales Press.

Desan, Christine (2014) *Making Money: Coin, Currency and the Coming of Capitalism*, Oxford: Oxford University Press.

Dietz, Rob and Dan O'Neill (2013) *Enough is Enough: Building a Sustainable Economy in a World of Finite Resources*, London: Routledge.

Dorling, Danny (2014) *Inequality and the 1%*, London: Verso.

Douthwaite, Richard (2000) *The Growth Illusion*, Dublin: Lilliput Press.

Douthwaite, Richard (1999) *The Ecology of Money*, Totnes: Green Books.

Douthwaite, Richard (1996) *Short Circuit: Strengthening Local Economies for Security in an Uncertain World*, Dublin: Lilliput Press.

Douthwaite, Richard and Danial Wagman (1999) *Barataria: A Community Exchange Network for the Third System*, Utrecht: Strohalm.

Dreze, Jean and Amartya Sen (2014) *An Uncertain Glory: India and its Contradictions*, London: Penguin.

Dryzek, John (with Simon Niemeyer) (2010) *Foundations and Frontiers of Deliberative Governance*, Oxford: Oxford University Press.

Eichengreen, Barry (2011) *Exorbitant Privilege*, Oxford: Oxford University Press.

Eichengreen, Barry (2008) *Globalizing Capital*, Princeton: Princeton University Press.

Epstein, Gerald (2013) 'Restructuring Finance to Better Serve Society', in Thomas I. Palley and Gustav A. Horn (eds) *Restoring Shared Prosperity: A Policy Agenda from Leading Keynesian Economists*, pp. 87–96, http://www.thomaspalley.com/docs/research/restoring_shared_prosperity.pdf

Erturk, Ismail and Stefano Solari (2007) 'Banks as Continuous Reinvention', *New Political Economy* 12:3, pp. 369–88.

Fuller, Duncan and Mary Mellor (2008) 'Banking on the Poor: Advancing Financial Inclusion in Newcastle upon Tyne UK', *Journal of Urban Studies* 45:7, pp. 1505–24.

Funnell, Warwick, Robert Jupe and Jane Andrew (2009) *In Government We Trust: Market Failure and the Delusions of Privatisation*, London: Pluto Press.

Galbraith, John Kenneth (1975) *Money: Whence it Came and Where it Went*, London: Penguin.

Ganssmann, Heiner (2011) *New Approaches to Monetary Theory*, London: Routledge.

Georgescu-Roegen, Nicolai (1971) *The Entropy Law and the Economic Process*, Cambridge, MA: Harvard University Press.

Giddens, Anthony (2000) *The Third Way and its Critics*, Cambridge: Polity.

Goodman, Halley (2009) 'The Formation of the Bank of England: A response to changing political and economic climate 1694', *Penn History Review* 17:1, pp. 10–30.

Graeber, David (2011) *Debt: The First 5,000 Years*, New York: Melville House Publishing.

Green New Deal Group (2008) *A Green New Deal*, http://www.neweconomics. org/sites/neweconomics.org/files/A_Green_New_Deal_1.pdf

Hahnel, Robin (2011) *Green Economics: Confronting the Ecological Crisis*, New York: ME Sharp.

Hanlon, Joseph, Armando Barrientos and David Hulme (2010) *Just Give Money to the Poor: The Development Revolution from the Global South*, Sterling, VA: Kumerian Press.

Harvey, David (2014) *Seventeen Contradictions and the End of Capitalism*, London: Profile Books.

Herndon, Thomas, Michael Ash and Robert Pollin (2014) 'Does High Public Debt Consistently Stifle Economic Growth? A critique of Reinhart and Rogoff', *Cambridge Journal of Economics* 38:2, pp. 257–79, http://www. oxfordjournals.org/page/5809/1

Hines, Colin (2000) *Localisation: A Global Manifesto*, London: Earthscan.

Hossein-zadeh, Ismael (2014) *Beyond Mainstream Explanations of the Financial Crisis: Parasitic Finance Capital*, London: Routledge.

Huber, Joseph (2014) 'Modern Money Theory and New Currency Theory', *real-world economics review* 66, pp. 38–57, http://www.paecon.net/ PAEReview/issue66/Huber66.pdf

Huber, Joseph and James Robertson (2000) *Creating New Money*, London: New Economics Foundation.

Hudson, Michael (2013) 'From the Bubble Economy to Debt Deflation and Privatization', *real-world economics review* 64, pp. 21–2, http://www.paecon.net/PAEReview/issue64/Hudson64.pdf

Huerta de Soto, Jesus (2010) 'Economic Recessions, Banking Reform and the Future of Capitalism', Hayek Memorial Lecture, London School of Economics, 28 October 2010.

Hutchinson, Frances, Mary Mellor and Wendy Olsen (2002) *The Politics of Money*, London: Pluto Press.

Illich, Ivan (1977) *The Right to Useful Employment*, London: Marion Boyars.

Ingham, Geoffrey (2004) *The Nature of Money*, Cambridge: Polity.

Innes, Mitchell A. (1914/2004) 'The Credit Theory of Money', in L. Randall Wray, *Credit and State Theories of Money: The Contribution of A. Mitchell Innes*, Cheltenham: Edward Elgar.

Innes, Mitchell A. (1913/2004) 'What is Money?', in L. Randall Wray, *Credit and State Theories of Money: The Contribution of A. Mitchell Innes*, Cheltenham: Edward Elgar.

Isla, Ana (2009) 'Who Pays for the Kyoto Protocol?', in Ariel Salleh (ed.) *Eco-Sufficiency and Global Justice*, London: Pluto Press.

Jackson, Andrew and Ben Dyson (2012) *Modernising Money*, London: Positive Money.

Jackson, Tim (2009) *Prosperity Without Growth?* London: Sustainable Development Commission.

Jones, Owen (2014) *The Establishment: And How They Get Away With It*, London: Allen Lane.

Keen, Steve (2013) 'A Bubble So Big We Can't Even See It', *real-world economics review* 64, pp. 3–10, http://www.paecon.net/PAEReview/issue64/Keen64.pdf

Keen, Steve (2011) *Debunking Economics: The Naked Emperor of the Social Sciences*, London: Zed/Pluto Press.

Keen, Steve (2009a) 'Bailing out the Titanic with a Thimble', *Economic Analysis and Policy* 39:1, pp. 3–24.

Keen, Steve (2009b) *Debtwatch* 31, February, www.debtdeflation.com/blogs

Keynes, John Maynard (1971) *A Treatise on Money: The Pure Theory of Money*, London: Macmillan.

King, John E. (2012) 'Post-Keynesians and Others', *Review of Political Economy* 24:2, pp. 305–19.

Klein, Naomi (2014) *This Changes Everything: Capitalism vs the Climate*, London: Allen Lane.

Knapp, G. F. (1924) *The State Theory of Money*, London: Macmillan.

Konings, Martjin (2009) 'Rethinking Neoliberalism and the Subprime Crisis: Beyond the reregulation agenda', *Competition and Change* 13:2, pp. 108–27.

Krugman, Paul (2012) *End this Depression Now*, New York: W. W. Norton.

Krugman, Paul (2008) *The Return of Depression Economics*, London: Penguin.

Kuhn, Thomas (1962) *The Structure of Scientific Revolutions*, Chicago: University of Chicago Press.

Lapavitsas, Costas (2013) *Profiting without Producing: How Finance Exploits Us All*, London: Verso.

Lapavitsas, Costas et al. (2012) *Crisis in the Eurozone*, London: Verso.

Large, Martin (2010) *Common Wealth: For a Free, Equal, Mutual and Sustainable Society*, Stroud: Hawthorn Press.

Latouche, Serge (2009) *Farewell to Growth*, Cambridge: Polity.

Lavoie, Marc (2011) 'Changes in Central Bank Procedures During the Subprime Crisis and their Repercussions on Monetary Theory', *International Journal of Political Economy* 39:3, pp. 3–23.

Lawson, Neal (2009) *All Consuming*, London: Penguin.

Lawson, Tony (1997) *Economics and Reality*, London: Routledge.

Lee, Fred (2012) 'Heterodox Economics and its Critics', *Review of Political Economy* 24:2, pp. 337–51.

Lerner, Abba (1943) 'Functional Finance and the Federal Debt', *Social Research* 10, pp. 38–51.

Lewis, Nathan (2007) *Gold: The Once and Future Money*, New Jersey: John Wiley and Sons.

Lietaer, Bernard (2001) *The Future of Money*, London: Century.

McMurtry, John (2002) *Value Wars: The Global Market Versus the Life Economy*, London: Pluto Press.

Martin, Felix (2014) *Money: The Unauthorised Biography*, London: Vintage.

Mazzucato, Mariana (2013) *The Entrepreneurial State: Debunking Public vs Private Sector Myths*, London: Anthem Press.

Meek, James (2014) *Private Island*, London: Verso.

Mellor, Mary (2014) 'Finance, War and Conflict', in Angie Zelter (ed.) *World in Chains*, Edinburgh: Luath Press.

Mellor, Mary (2013) 'The Unsustainability of Economic Man', *Okologisches Wirtschaften* 4, pp. 30–3.

Mellor, Mary (2012a) 'Money as a Public Resource for Development', *Development* 55:1, pp. 45–53.

Mellor, Mary (2012b) 'Co-operative Principles for a Green Economy', *Journal of the Society for Co-operative Studies* 45:1, pp. 5–14.

Mellor, Mary (2010a) *The Future of Money: From Financial Crisis to Public Resource*, London: Pluto Press.

Mellor, Mary (2010b) 'Could the Money System be the Basis of a Sufficiency Economy?', *real-world economics review* 54, pp. 79–88, http://www.paecon. net/PAERevuew/issue54/Mellor54.pdf

Mellor, Mary (2009) 'Ecofeminist Political Economy and the Politics of Money', in Ariel Salleh (ed.) *Eco-Sufficiency and Global Justice*, London: Pluto Press.

Mellor, Mary (1997) 'Women, Nature and the Social Construction of "Economic Man"', *Ecological Economics* 20:2, pp. 129–40.

Mies, Maria (1998) *Patriarchy and Accumulation on a World Scale*, London: Zed Books.

Montgomerie, Johnna and Karel Williams (2009) 'Financialised Capitalism: After the crisis and beyond neoliberalism', *Competition and Change* 13:2, pp. 99–107.

Nadal, Alejandro (2011) *Rethinking Macroeconomics for Sustainability*, London: Zed Books.

Nelson, Anitra and Frans Timmerman (eds) (2011) *Life Without Money*, London: Pluto Press.

Nersisyan, Yeva and L. Randall Wray (2010) 'Deficit Hysteria Redux? Why we should stop worrying about US government deficits', *real-world economics review* 53, pp. 109–28.

Nesvetailova, Anastasia (2007) *Fragile Finance: Debt, Speculation and Crisis in an Age of Global Credit*, Basingstoke: Palgrave Macmillan.

North, Peter (2007) *Money and Liberation*, Minneapolis: University of Minnesota Press.

Nylen, William R. (2003) *Participatory Democracy versus Elitist Democracy*, Basingstoke: Palgrave Macmillan.

Ozgur, Gokcer and Korkut A. Erturk (2008) 'Endogneous Money in the Age of Financial Liberalization', Working Paper No. 2008-6, University of Utah.

Palley, Thomas I. (2013a) 'The War of Ideas: A Comparison of the US and Europe', in Thomas I. Palley and Gustav A. Horn (eds) *Restoring Shared Prosperity: A Policy Agenda from Leading Keynesian Economists*, pp. 7–14, http://www.thomaspalley.com/docs/research/restoring_shared_ prosperity.pdf

Palley, Thomas I. (2013b) 'Making Finance Serve the Real Economy', in Thomas I. Palley and Gustav A. Horn (eds) *Restoring Shared Prosperity: A Policy Agenda from Leading Keynesian Economists*, pp. 73–80, http://www. thomaspalley.com/docs/research/restoring_shared_prosperity.pdf

Palley, Thomas I. and Gustav A. Horn (eds) (2013) *Restoring Shared Prosperity: A Policy Agenda from Leading Keynesian Economists*, http:// www.thomaspalley.com/docs/research/restoring_shared_prosperity.pdf

Panayotakis, Costas (2011) *Remaking Scarcity: From Capitalist Inefficiency to Economic Democracy*, London: Pluto Press.

Parguez, Alain and Mario Seccareccia (2000) 'The Credit Theory of Money: The Money Circuit Approach', in John Smithin (ed.) *What is Money?*, London: Routledge.

Peet, R. (2009) *Unholy Trinity: The IMF, World Bank and WTO*, London: Zed Books.

Piketty, Thomas (2014) *Capital in the 21st Century*, Cambridge, MA: Harvard University Press.

Polanyi, Karl (1944/57) *The Great Transformation*, Boston: Beacon Press.

Pollin, Robert (2013) 'Short- and Long-Run Alternatives to Austerity in the US', in Thomas I. Palley and Gustav A. Horn (eds) *Restoring Shared Prosperity: A Policy Agenda from Leading Keynesian Economists*, pp. 63–70, http://www.thomaspalley.com/docs/research/restoring_shared_prosperity.pdf

Power, Marilyn (2004) 'Social Provisioning as a Starting Point for Feminist Economics', *Feminist Economics* 10:3, pp. 3–19.

Prasad, Eswar (2014) *The Dollar Trap*, Princeton: Princeton University Press.

Quiggin, John (2010) *Zombie Economics: How Dead Ideas Still Walk Among Us*, Princeton: Princeton University Press.

Raddon Mary-Beth (2003) *Community and Money*, Montreal: Black Rose Books.

Read, Rupert (2014) 'Post-Growth Common Sense', in John Blewitt and Ray Cunningham (eds) *The Post-Growth Project*, London: Green House London Publishing Partnership.

Reinhart, Carmen and Kenneth Rogoff (2010) 'Growth in Time of Debt', NBER Working Paper 15639, January 2010, http://www.nber.org/papers/w15639

Rickards, James (2011) *Currency Wars: The Making of the Next Global Crisis*, New York: Portfolio/Penguin.

Robertson, James (2012) *Future Money: Breakdown or Breakthrough?* Totnes: Green Books.

Robertson, James (1985) *Future Work*, London: Temple Smith/Gower.

Robertson, James and John M. Bunzl (2003) *Monetary Reform: Making it Happen!*, London: ISPO.

Rossi, Sergio (2007) *Money and Payments in Theory and Practice*, London: Routledge.

Rowbotham, Michael (2000) *Goodbye America! Globalisation, Debt and the Dollar Empire*, Charlebury: Jon Carpenter.

Ryan-Collins, Josh, Tony Greenham, Richard Werner and Andrew Jackson (2011) *Where Does Money Come From? A Guide to the UK Monetary and Banking System*, London: New Economics Foundation.

Salleh, Ariel (ed.) (2009) *Eco-sufficiency and Global Justice: Women Write Political Ecology*, London: Pluto Press.

Sayer, Andrew (2014) *Why We Can't Afford the Rich*, Bristol: Policy Press.

Scurlock, James D. (2007) *Maxed Out: Hard Times, Easy Credit*, London: HarperCollins.

Seyfang, Gillian (2011) *The New Economics of Sustainable Consumption: Seeds of Change*, Basingstoke Palgrave Macmillan.

Schumacher, Fritz (1973) *Small is Beautiful: Economics as if People Mattered*, London: Abacus.

Shiva, Vandana (2012) *Making Peace with the Earth*, London: Pluto Press.

Silvers, Damon (2013) 'The Financial System, Financialization and the Path to Economic Recovery', in Thomas I. Palley and Gustav A. Horn (eds) *Restoring Shared Prosperity: A Policy Agenda from Leading Keynesian Economists*, pp. 97–104, http://www.thomaspalley.com/docs/research/restoring_shared_prosperity

Skidelsky, Robert and Edward Skidelsky (2012) *How Much is Enough? The Love of Money, and the Case for the Good Life*, London: Allen Lane.

Smithin, John (2009) *Money, Enterprise and Income Distribution*, London: Routledge.

Soddy, Frederick (1926) *Wealth, Virtual Wealth and Debt*, London: Allen and Unwin.

Stiglitz, Joseph (2010) *Freefall: Free Markets and the Sinking of the Global Economy*, London: Allen Lane.

Stiglitz J. E. and Bruce Greenwald (2009) 'A Modest Proposal for International Monetary Reform', Initiative for Policy Dialogue Working Paper Series, http://academiccommons.columbia.edu/catalog/ac:154006

Streeck, Wolfgang (2014) 'How Will Capitalism End?', *New Left Review* 87, May–June, pp. 35–56.

Swift, Richard (2014) 'Stop the Gold Rush', *New Internationalist* 475, September, pp. 12–16.

Taub, Jennifer (2013) 'Delays, Dilutions, and Delusions: Implementing the Dodd-Frank Act', in Thomas I. Palley and Gustav A. Horn (eds) *Restoring Shared Prosperity: A Policy Agenda from Leading Keynesian Economists*, pp. 105–12, http://www.thomaspalley.com/docs/research/restoring_shared_prosperity.pdf

Tobin, J (1963) 'Commercial Banks and Creators of Money', in D. Carson (ed.) *Banking and Monetary Studies*, Homewood, IL: Unwin.

United Nations and Asian Development Bank (2012) *Green Growth, Resources and Resilience: Environmental Sustainability in Asia and the Pacific*, http://www.adb.org/sites/default/files/green-growth-resources-resilience.pdf

Varoufakis, Yanis (2011) *The Global Minotaur*, London: Zed Books.

Waring, Marilyn (1989) *If Women Counted*, Basingstoke: Macmillan.

Weeks, John (2014) *Economics of the 1%*, London: Anthem Other Canon Economics.

Wheatley, Alan (ed.) (2013) *The Power of Currencies and the Currencies of Power*, London: Routledge.

Wilkinson, Richard and Kate Pickett (2010) *The Spirit Level: Why Equality is Better for Everyone*, London: Penguin.

Wolf, Martin (2014) *The Shifts and the Shocks: What We've Learned and Have Still to Learn From the Financial Crisis*, London: Allen Lane.

Wray, L. Randall (2012) *Modern Money Theory*, Basingstoke: Palgrave Macmillan.

Wray, L. Randall (2011) *Keynes After 75 years: Rethinking Money as a Public Monopoly*, Working Paper No. 658, Levy Institute, Bard College, Annandale-on-Hudson, New York.

Wray, L. Randall (2009) *The Return of Big Government: Policy Advice for President Obama*, Public Policy Brief No. 99, Levy Institute, Bard College, Annandale-on-Hudson, New York.

Wray, L. Randall (2004) 'Conclusion: The Credit Money and State Money Approaches', in L. Randall Wray (ed.) *Credit and State Theories of Money: The Contribution of A. Mitchell Innes*, Cheltenham: Edward Elgar.

Zelizer, Viviana (1994) *The Social Meaning of Money*, New York: Basic Books.

Index

Compiled by Sue Carlton